GLOBALIZATION, POLITICS, AND FINANCIAL TURMOIL

ASIA'S BANKING CRISIS

In a world where capital moves freely across national borders, developing countries have increasingly been subjected to devastating financial crises caused by the sudden withdrawal of foreign capital. How do such crises come about? This book focuses on a novel causal path: that of miscommunication. It demonstrates how and why developing democracies are exceptionally vulnerable to breakdowns in communication between financial officials and the chief executive through a close examination of Asia's financial crisis of 1997–8, and it outlines the disastrous consequences of such breakdowns.

Shanker Satyanath is currently an assistant professor in the Department of Politics at New York University. He received his Masters in management from Northwestern University and his Ph.D. in political science from Columbia University.

POLITICAL ECONOMY OF INSTITUTIONS AND DECISIONS

Series Editors

Randall Calvert, *Washington University, St. Louis*
Thrainn Eggertsson, *Max Planck Institute, Germany, and University of Iceland*

Founding Editors

James E. Alt, *Harvard University*
Douglass C. North, *Washington University, St. Louis*

Other Books in the Series

Alberto Alesina and Howard Rosenthal, *Partisan Politics, Divided Government and the Economy*
Lee J. Alston, Thrainn Eggertsson, and Douglass C. North, eds., *Empirical Studies in Institutional Change*
Lee J. Alston and Joseph P. Ferrie, *Southern Paternalism and the Rise of the American Welfare State: Economics, Politics, and Institutions, 1865–1965*
James E. Alt and Kenneth Shepsle, eds., *Perspectives on Positive Political Economy*
Josephine T. Andrews, *When Majorities Fail: The Russian Parliament, 1990–1993*
Jeffrey S. Banks and Eric A. Hanushek, eds., *Modern Political Economy: Old Topics, New Directions*
Yoram Barzel, *Economic Analysis of Property Rights*, 2nd edition
Yoram Barzel, *A Theory of the State: Economic Rights, Legal Rights, and the Scope of the State*
Robert Bates, *Beyond the Miracle of the Market: The Political Economy of Agrarian Development in Kenya*, 2nd edition
Kelly H. Chang, *Appointing Central Bankers: The Politics of Monetary Policy in the United States and the European Monetary Union*
Peter Cowhey and Mathew McCubbins, eds., *Structure and Policy in Japan and the United States*
Gary W. Cox, *The Efficient Secret: The Cabinet and the Development of Political Parties in Victorian England*
Gary W. Cox, *Making Votes Count: Strategic Coordination in the World's Electoral Systems*

Continued on page following index

GLOBALIZATION, POLITICS, AND FINANCIAL TURMOIL

Asia's Banking Crisis

SHANKER SATYANATH

New York University

CAMBRIDGE
UNIVERSITY PRESS

CAMBRIDGE UNIVERSITY PRESS
Cambridge, New York, Melbourne, Madrid, Cape Town, Singapore, São Paulo

Cambridge University Press
40 West 20th Street, New York, NY 10011-4211, USA

www.cambridge.org
Information on this title: www.cambridge.org/9780521854924

First published 2006

Printed in the United States of America

A catalog record for this publication is available from the British Library.

Library of Congress Cataloging in Publication Data
Satyanath, Shanker
Globalization, politics, and financial turmoil : Asia's banking crisis / Shanker Satyanath.
p. cm. – (Political economy of institutions and decisions)
Includes bibliographical references and index.
ISBN 0-521-85492-X (hardback)
1. Banks and banking – Asia. 2. Capital movements – Asia.
3. Bank management – Asia. 4. Banking law – Asia. 5. Financial crises – Asia.
I. Title. II. Series
HG3252.S27 2006
332.1′0959 – dc22   2005000639

ISBN-13   978-0-521-85492-4 hardback
ISBN-10   0-521-85492-X hardback

To my family

Contents

Figures and Tables

FIGURES

TABLES

Preface

We now live in a world where capital often moves freely across national borders. In this world, developing countries have increasingly been subjected to devastating financial crises caused by the sudden withdrawal of foreign capital. These crises have had severe humanitarian consequences; in East Asia in 1997–98 some countries experienced economic contractions comparable to levels seen in the Great Depression. How do such crises come about? I focus on a novel causal path, that of miscommunication. I demonstrate why developing democracies are exceptionally vulnerable to breakdowns in communication between financial officials and the chief executive. These breakdowns have disastrous consequences because they result in inadequate bank regulation, which encourages the withdrawal of foreign capital.

This book contributes to three literatures. The first is the literature on globalization of capital. This literature has hitherto paid little attention to how globalization can have disastrous consequences in political environments where there are problems in the credible communication of financial information, and this is a contribution of my book. The second is the literature on the politics of financial crises. It is plausible that the presence of ill-informed chief executives raises the likelihood of financial crises. However, scholars of crises have hitherto been unable to systematically identify where we are likely to observe an ill-informed chief executive, thanks to the absence of any preexisting analytical framework for such an analysis. This book offers a framework for all scholars of crises to use when predicting where chief executives are likely to be ill informed about critical economic variables. Finally, the book also contributes to the booming literature on veto players, actors whose approval is necessary for policy change. The standard pathology of multiple veto players identified by this literature is policy stagnation. This book is the first to identify a new pathology. By showing that the presence of multiple veto players can damage the flow of accurate information between financial officials and politicians, the book demonstrates a fresh causal path from multiple veto players to catastrophic financial crises.

This book represents a unique opportunity for me to bring together what I have learned from my past in the world of international business, my immersion in the political economy of development, and my fascination with incomplete information game theory. When I started out as a graduate student at Columbia I could hardly have predicted that such an eclectic mix of knowledge could cohere in any one work. It was first Helen Milner, and subsequently Walter Mattli and Mark Kesselman, who took me under their wings and convinced me that this was possible. Frederic Mishkin, Prajit Dutta, and Raghu Sundaram convinced me that my findings were also of great interest to economists. It is to them and to my NYU colleagues, Bruce Bueno de Mesquita, Adam Przeworski, Steven Brams, Bill Clark, Mike Gilligan, and Alastair Smith, who provided invaluable advice at critical moments, that I owe the most for completing this project.

Other colleagues at NYU also helped me a great deal. I am extremely thankful to Dimitri Landa, Bumba Mukherjee, Leonard Wantchekon, Lawrence Broz, Sandy Gordon, Fiona McGillivary, Jonathan Nagler, George Downs, Becky Morton, Marek Kaminski, Cathy Hafer, David Denoon, and Libby Wood for reading numerous versions of the argument. Outside New York University, Abraham Kim, Eric Neher, Clark Neher, John Huber, Jon Elster, Erik Gartzke, Stephan Haggard, Andrew MacIntyre, and Stathis Kalyvas also provided useful advice. Cayetano Paderanga opened numerous doors for me in the Philippines, as did Dr. Jeyaratnam and Nandini Jeyaratnam in Malaysia, and Narayan and Shreemati Menon in Indonesia. I would also like to thank the series editor and two reviewers, all of whom gave the manuscript remarkably close readings and provided numerous helpful suggestions, as well as Lewis Bateman, Ciara McLaughlin, Eric Schwartz, and Elise Oranges, all of whom made working with Cambridge an absolute pleasure.

I would like to also thank my family and friends for their constant support. Chuck Mee was the first to point out that my intellectual curiosity would be best satisfied in a large university setting. My late father, T. C. Satyanath's, intellectual energy served as a constant motivating force, while my mother, Sudha Bhasi, and my closest relatives, Vikram Satyanath, Smita Satyanath, Amala Pothen, Susie Mee, and Ashwini Bhasi, encouraged every stage of my academic development. Jack Fentress and Andy Striso helped me tide over the lifestyle transition from businessman to graduate student. Finally, my debts to my wife Erin and my daughter Leila are too deep to put down on paper.

GLOBALIZATION, POLITICS, AND FINANCIAL TURMOIL

ASIA'S BANKING CRISIS

1

Introduction

On July 2, 1997, Rerngchai Marakanond, the governor of the Thai central bank, announced that he did not control sufficient foreign reserves to defend his country's currency from speculative attacks. Whereas Asia had been an exceptionally popular destination for international capital in the mid-1990s, this date marked a decisive turning point in lenders' confidence in the region's economic prospects. International lenders began to shift their funds out of Asia in vast quantities. In countries where there were few rules restricting the movement of capital across borders, the outflow of capital was especially astounding. In the second half of 1997 alone capital outflows from these countries amounted to at least $34 billion.[1] The currencies of many of these countries were subjected to devaluations of 40–80% in a matter of months, precipitating the collapse of several banking sectors and causing economic contractions of up to 15 percent of the gross domestic product.[2]

In accounting for this crisis some scholars have focused on the dangers of allowing the liberal inflow of short-term loans; because such loans can be withdrawn rapidly, heavy exposure to these loans renders economies exceptionally vulnerable to sudden shifts in market sentiments. For these scholars the fundamental lesson to be learned from the Asian crisis is that developing countries should retain controls on international capital flows.[3] However, other scholars have argued that the root causes of the crisis go far deeper. These scholars have focused on the failure of many Asian countries with limited restrictions on capital flows to have stringent

---

[1] Radelet and Sachs 1998, 6.
[2] Goldstein 1998, 2 and Bank Negara 1998a.
[3] See Bhagwati 1998, Rodrik 1998, Wade and Veneroso 1998, Furman and Stiglitz 1998.

1

prudential bank regulatory environments, defined as environments where regulators enforce strict rules aimed at safeguarding the solvency of banks.[4] For these scholars the fundamental lesson to be learned from the Asian crisis is not that capital flows should be controlled; rather, it is that stringent prudential bank regulation is critical to the viability of the liberal capital flows/open capital account strategy.[5] Opponents of liberal capital flows remain unconvinced that a shift to stringent prudential regulation would come close to rendering capital flow liberalization viable in the developing world.[6]

Although the two sides of the debate appear to be caught in a deadlock, there is indeed an area of agreement. Even supporters of liberalization agree that incredible long-term commitments to stringent prudential bank regulation are extremely dangerous under liberal capital flows.[7] However, contributors to the debate have not systematically identified which *political* environments make it difficult to credibly commit to stringent regulation for the long term. Given that the downside from capital flow liberalization can be extreme, identifying such environments is of critical importance to academics and policy makers alike. Furthermore, given that the Asian experience with liberalization in the 1990s encompasses the lion's share of developing countries that have chosen to operate in liberal capital environments in recent years, it is especially important to dissect the Asian experience to advance our knowledge in this area.

In this book I identify political environments that are relatively likely to embody incredible long-term commitments to stringent bank regulation. I do so by applying the tools of game theory to an analysis of bank regulation under liberal capital flows in Asia in the years leading up to the 1997 currency crisis. The primary contribution of this book is to identify a causal path to weak regulation in the developing world that has so far escaped notice. This path takes account of the fact that, in technically complex financial issue areas, chief executives generally base their decisions on signals received from their senior financial advisors.

---

[4] As defined by Dewatripont and Tirole "the main concern of prudential bank regulation is the solvency of banks, namely the relation between equity, debt, and asset riskiness." See Dewatripont and Tirole 1994, 5.

[5] Eichengreen 1998, 8 offers the most coherent defense of this position.

[6] See Rodrik 1998b.

[7] Eichengreen 1998 goes so far as to make such commitments a pre-condition for liberal capital flows.

I show that when these advisors have policy preferences which differ from that of the chief executive they have incentives to be vague about the state of the banking sector. This means that even a chief executive who would like to regulate banks stringently is vulnerable to underregulating banks because he is not precisely informed of the true state of vulnerability of the banks. The question then is, what are the political conditions under which lax regulation through the above causal path is most likely to occur?

I demonstrate that in the developing world it is democracies that are most likely to be vulnerable to lax regulation by miscommunication. I argue that when this novel causal path to lax regulation is taken into account, along with other causal paths that have already been identified in the crisis literature, the conclusion is clear. Developing-country democracies are exceptionally ill suited to operating under liberal capital flows from the perspective of bank regulation. This conclusion is new to the literature on capital flow liberalization in the developing world.

Note that I do not consider the above causal path to be the only one leading to lax regulation. It is only one of three paths, two of which have already received attention in the crisis literature. I argue that a failure to meet any one of the following political conditions in developing-country contexts results in an incredible long-term commitment to stringent regulation under liberal capital flows. These conditions are

a. Freedom for the chief executive to appoint an official who shares his regulatory preferences to the apex of the financial bureaucracy, which I call the *signaling condition*.
b. A chief executive without personal financial ties to the banking sector, which I call the *anti-cronyism condition*.
c. Delegation of adequate regulatory powers to the executive branch, which I call the *anti-gridlock condition*.

The logic relating failure to meet the anti-cronyism and anti-gridlock conditions to lax regulation is straightforward and already well understood. Failure to meet the anti-cronyism condition results in lax regulation because the chief executive has weak incentives for stringent regulation. Failure to meet the anti-gridlock condition results in lax regulation because essential regulatory reforms may be blocked by the legislature. The novel signaling condition derives from a key finding from the theory of "cheap talk" signaling – that a small difference in preferences between a sender and a receiver of signals generates vagueness in the signals sent by the former to the latter. This vagueness is strategic in nature, in that it is aimed at misleading the receiver into advancing the sender's priorities. Henceforth I refer to the vagueness in communication that results from even a small difference in preferences as the signaling problem for bank regulation. I claim that in the developing world it is democracies rather than authoritarian regimes that cannot credibly commit to always having a solution to the signaling problem. The logic that underpins this claim is as follows.

The chief executive can avoid having a signaling problem if he appoints adequately skilled relatives, close friends, or long-time associates who share his (the chief executive's) regulatory preferences to senior positions from which they can monitor regulatory information that is private to the government. Because these officials share the chief executive's preferences, they do not have incentives to deceive the chief executive. In authoritarian regimes, almost by definition, the legislature does not serve as a check on the chief executive's power to make such appointments. In democracies, however, appointments to the apex of the financial bureaucracy often have to be approved by the legislature. Chief executives of democracies are thus far less assured of being able to find a solution to the signaling problem than chief executives of authoritarian regimes. Democracies are thus likely to find it exceptionally difficult to make credible long-term commitments to avoiding lax regulation caused by strategic miscommunication.

This finding has powerful implications. Since the anti-gridlock condition is likely to be fulfilled in an authoritarian environment, an authoritarian country's long-term commitment to stringent regulation is likely to be credible in the presence of a chief executive who does not have personal financial ties to the banking sector. However, a democratic developing country's long-term commitment to stringent regulation is likely to be incredible thanks to signaling issues even in the presence of a chief executive who does not have close personal financial ties to the banking sector. This is the case even if we assume the anti-gridlock condition to be fulfilled.

Note that I am careful to limit my claims to the realm of developing countries. This is so because there is an alternative solution to the signaling problem, namely, the chief executive simply relinquishes decision-making authority to an independent regulatory bureaucracy. While I am unable to identify a single bank regulatory bureaucracy that is genuinely insulated from politicians in the developing world, this solution often

4

prevails in the developed world.[8] I thus limit my claims to environments where regulatory independence is absent, that is, to the developing world.

I also limit my claim to countries that are operating without the benefit of substantial controls on capital flows. This is the case because the formal signaling model assumes a background environment in which the banking sector is always vulnerable to substantial exogenous shocks to loan default rates. This may often not be the case for economies where capital flows are tightly restricted.

I begin this chapter by briefly summarizing the current literature bearing on variations in bank regulation in Asia under liberal capital flows. I then outline my argument and address alternative arguments. Finally, I offer an overview of the structure of this book.

1.1 THE LITERATURE ON VARIATIONS IN BANK REGULATION

To date there have been few systematic attempts at explaining variations in prudential bank regulation in Asia under liberal capital flows from a political perspective. However, some of the literature on the Asian crisis generates implications that offer us some testable predictions. The theories that could potentially account for these variations may be divided into two categories: preference-driven and institution-driven.

Preference-driven theories focus on the presence or absence of evidence of financial ties between chief executives and bank owners. Where such evidence is present, the chief executive is dubbed a *crony capitalist*. Where there is no evidence of such ties, the chief executive is considered to have arm's length relations with bank owners. Lax regulation is attributed to the presence of "cronyistic" chief executives who preferred lax regulation because it offered them and/or their crony bank owners immense financial rewards. (See, for instance, the work of Michael Backman.[9]) President Soeharto of Indonesia serves as the prototypical crony capitalist in such explanations. While providing important insights, this strand of the literature fails to take account of the fact that in some political environments chief executives may be institutionally constrained from implementing their preferred policies by the presence of other powerful

---

[8] In the developing world, Chile is a possible lone exception, which I discuss in the concluding chapter.

[9] Backman 1999.

actors with opposed preferences. Thus, as I will show shortly, stringent regulation does not directly follow from the absence of a cronyistic chief executive.

The second strand of the literature, what I term as institution-driven, uses the well-known concept of veto players. Veto players are actors whose assent is required for shifts in policy from the status quo.[10] The number of veto players is seen to capture the degree of checks on the chief executive's power. A political environment with numerous coalition parties in the cabinet (high checks on the chief executive's power) is an environment with a large number of veto players. On the opposite pole, a political environment with few checks on the chief executive's power is an environment with very few veto players. A democratic political environment where the chief executive is not operating in a fragmented coalition (intermediate checks) is an environment with a moderate number of veto players.

Andrew MacIntyre is the primary exponent of veto player theory in the context of the Asian crisis.[11] MacIntyre focuses on how four South East Asian countries responded to the 1997–98 financial crisis.[12] He reconciles two strands of the broad political economy literature on the centralization/fragmentation of power, one of which emphasizes the benefits of added credibility of commitments under fragmentation and another that emphasizes the dangers of policy gridlock under such conditions.[13] He argues that two types of countries are likely to display poor governance. First, countries where political power is highly fragmented (i.e., there are many checks on the chief executive's power) are likely to face problems of policy gridlock that stand in the way of resolving crises. This is the case because the approval of many actors is required for any policy change. Second, countries where political power is highly centralized (i.e., there are very few checks on the chief executive's power) are likely to face problems in credibly committing to good governance in response to crises. This is the case because there are no additional veto players who are present to block a dictator from reneging from good governance. He concludes that countries where political power is neither overly centralized nor fragmented, that is, where there are moderate checks on the chief executive's power, are most likely to display good governance because

[10] Tsebelis 2000.
[11] MacIntyre 2001 and 2002.
[12] The four countries are the Philippines, Thailand, Malaysia, and Indonesia.
[13] North and Weingast (1989) and Keefer (2002) emphasize the benefits of institutional checks and balances, while McCubbins (1991) and Roubini and Sachs (1989) emphasize the dangers of gridlock under such conditions.

they are likely to be spared the problems of excessive gridlock as well as incredible commitments to good governance.

Although MacIntyre's argument is directed at explaining responses to crises, including bank regulatory responses, his theory has obvious implications for where we should and should not expect to see credible commitments to stringent prudential bank regulation in noncrisis periods. The World Bank has conducted a study of the overall quality of bank regulatory environments in Asian countries with liberal capital flows, which makes an assessment of these implications possible.[14] The data were collected in 1997, *prior* to the implementation of post-crisis reforms; thus, they reasonably accurately reflect the state of bank regulation in these countries in the 1990s prior to the currency crisis. These data can thus be used as indicators of the stringency of bank regulation in Asia between capital flow liberalization, which mostly occurred in the early 1990s, and the Asian crisis, which is the focus of this book. The data offer conclusions that differ from the implications of MacIntyre's purely institutional theory, most prominently in indicating that some countries with very few checks on the chief executive's power were able to commit to stringent bank regulation, while countries with a moderate number of checks failed to do so. The data are also inconsistent with a purely preference-driven theory, most notably in showing that Thailand and the Philippines failed to have stringent regulatory environments in the wake of liberalization despite the fact that their chief executives upon liberalization (Chuan Leekpai and Fidel Ramos) were by no means Soeharto-style crony capitalists (Figure 1.1).

In the next section I offer an overview of my argument, which accounts for these variations.

1.2 MY ARGUMENT IN BRIEF

In this book I add an informational and a strategic component to our understanding of the variations described above. The main claims of this book can be summarized in two tables. Table 1.1 displays my claim that the presence of insignificant (very few) checks on a chief executive's power to make appointments to the apex of the financial bureaucracy is a necessary but not sufficient condition for a credible long-term commitment to stringent regulation. Since it is chief executives in democratic regimes who are most likely to face significant checks to their power, democratic

[14] Caprio 1998.

Figure 1.1 Prudential bank regulatory environments and the degree of checks. In this figure, I follow MacIntyre's classification of Indonesia and Malaysia as countries with very few checks, the Philippines as a country with moderate checks, and Thailand as a country with many checks. For South Korea and Singapore, which were not evaluated by MacIntyre, I use the World Bank's assessment of checks (Beck et al. 2001). As per the World Bank, Singapore had two checks, which placed it close to Indonesia (one check), while South Korea had three to four checks, which placed it short of Thailand (six checks). Neither MacIntyre nor the World Bank rate Hong Kong. Based on a study of the regional literature, I classify Hong Kong, a British colony during the period analyzed here, as a country where there were few local checks on the power of the governor. (See Chapter 6 for details.) The World Bank's scale for bank regulatory environments has five categories. I have numbered these categories such that more stringent regulation gets a higher category score. (I provide more details about this scale in Appendix 1.)

regimes are relatively ill suited to operating under liberal capital flows from the perspective of bank regulation (Table 1.1).

Table 1.1 shows that I expect regulatory outcomes to be in line with the chief executive's crony contacts in environments with insignificant checks. Where the chief executive has cronyistic ties to bank owners, I claim the environment is prone to lax regulation. Where the chief executive has arms' length relations with bank owners, I claim the environment is not prone to lax regulation. In environments with significant checks, however, I claim that the propensity for lax regulation remains even if the chief executive does not have cronyistic ties to bank owners.

I attribute the difference between environments with insignificant and significant checks to the fact that the latter environments are exceptionally vulnerable to failing to find a solution to the signaling problem as well as to policy gridlock (see Table 1.2).

I first summarize my arguments for why democracies are exceptionally vulnerable to the signaling problem. (I emphasize that my point is not that democracies will always have signaling problems, but rather that they are more vulnerable to them than authoritarian regimes.) I then provide an overview of the reasons why democratic regimes are exceptionally vulnerable to gridlock.

8

Table 1.1 *Chief Executives' Preferences, Institutional Environments, and the Credibility of Long-Term Commitments to Stringent Regulation*

	Insignificant Checks	Significant Checks
Chief executive has bank owner cronies	Incredible	Incredible
Chief executive does not have bank owner cronies	Credible	Incredible

Table 1.2 *Chief Executives' Preferences, Institutional Environments, and Vulnerability to Signaling and Gridlock Problems*

	Insignificant Checks	Significant Checks
Chief executive has bank owner cronies	Not vulnerable to signaling or gridlock problems	Vulnerable to signaling and gridlock problems
Chief executive does not have bank owner cronies	Not vulnerable to signaling or gridlock problems	Vulnerable to signaling and gridlock problems

1.2.1 The Signaling Problem in Democratic Environments

I begin by classifying bank regulatory environments according to their stringency. Arguably the most critical aspect of the stringency of the bank regulatory environment is bank capital relative to loan defaults. (See Appendix 1 for other aspects.) This is the case because in bank accounting a shortfall of shareholder capital relative to loan defaults means a bank is technically insolvent. Thus, a bank/banking sector for which capital falls short of expected loan defaults would be weak, that is, less than moderately robust. A reasonable way to define a moderately stringent prudential bank regulatory environment would be to say that such an environment is one in which the government always responds to jumps in expected loan defaults by ensuring that the banking sector has sufficient shareholder capital to cover the defaults, that is, the government always ensures that the banking sector is at least moderately robust following its regulatory response. Failure to always do so would plausibly indicate that the bank regulatory environment is lax.

I now address the preferences of officials with regard to banking sector robustness. It is generally costly for banks to raise capital. Bank owners thus have incentives to maintain as low a capital base as possible alongside a guarantee of survival from the government. If an official has cronyistic (i.e., personal financial) ties to bank owners, this would give him incentives to allow banks to maintain capital levels below defaults in anticipation of an eventual government bailout. This would amount to a preference for a banking sector that is less than moderately robust. However, if an official does not have such cronyistic ties, there is little reason for him to have a preference for anything less than a moderately robust banking sector. I show in the following paragraphs why, under conditions of incomplete and asymmetric information, democratic political environments are vulnerable to lax regulation even when the chief executive does not have cronyistic ties to bank owners.

Why is it important to use a framework with incomplete and asymmetric information? Whereas public information abounds about several aspects of the banking sector, the precise sector-wide level of expected loan defaults is generally not common knowledge. This is the case because accounting practices in developing countries are exceptionally opaque, and many banks are not subject to private sector ratings. For instance, banks often loan money to defaulting lenders for the purpose of making minimum loan payments, and thus mask defaults. It is very hard to gauge the precise degree to which banks have engaged in this practice without closely examining banks' accounts. (Whereas rumors may abound, there is no good way to assess their veracity.) Precise information about sector-wide expected defaults is only likely to be accessible to technically skilled officials who are authorized to closely examine banks' accounts, that is, the officials who are responsible for bank supervision. Given that the chief executive must be concerned with many issues other than bank regulation, and is also generally technically untrained in deciphering banks' accounts, he is highly unlikely to have direct access to this information. If the chief executive wants to be precisely informed about expected defaults, he must generally rely on the officials who are responsible for bank supervision to signal this information to him prior to making important regulatory decisions.

The officials who ultimately control the bank supervisory bureaucracy are one or both of the senior-most members of the financial bureaucracy, the central bank governor and the finance minister. What are the consequences of having a central bank governor/finance minister with preferences over banking sector robustness that are different from the chief executive? First, consider the simple case in which the central bank governor does not report to the finance minister; thus the governor is the only official signaler of information collected by bank supervisors on the level of expected defaults. The situation is one in which the chief executive ultimately decides on the amount of capital that banks must maintain after observing a signal from the governor on the level of expected defaults. (Recall that central bank governors are generally not independent of politicians in the developing world.) Note that robustness is the difference between capital and expected defaults, and the goal of the chief executive is to end up with a level of robustness at his ideal level.

As mentioned, the theory of "cheap talk" signaling indicates that even a small difference in preferences between the sender and receiver of signals generates incentives for vagueness on the part of the sender. Furthermore, there is a threshold distance in preferences between the sender and receiver at which the sender has incentives to not just be vague, but to be completely uninformative. The equilibrium when the threshold is met takes the form in which the chief executive, believing that the governor is not providing any useful information, ignores the governor's signals. Anticipating that the chief executive will ignore his signals, the central bank governor loses nothing by providing completely useless information, and the vicious circle is complete because the chief executive's beliefs are justified. In Chapter 3, I will show that the threshold difference in preferences between the chief executive and the central bank governor at which completely uninformative signaling occurs is fairly small in the realm of bank regulation. (Completely uninformative signaling starts as a difference of opinion over the ideal level of capital that banks must keep as a buffer over expected defaults of just 4 percentage points.)

The consequence of having a governor with different preferences from the chief executive is that the chief executive does not have adequate access to the most precise information on default levels, that collected by bank supervisors from site visits to banks.[15] The chief executive may be able to gain some information on defaults from the financial press. However, the press in the developing world is notoriously unreliable when it comes to private financial information, meaning that this source is hardly an adequate substitute for information collected by bank supervisors.

This leaves us with two sets of solutions to the signaling problem. One is for the chief executive to appoint an official who shares his preferences

---

[15] The plausible assumption is that the central bank governor, as the head of the supervisory bureaucracy, maintains some control over the flow of information from supervisors.

to the central bank governorship. The second is for him to supercede the conventional bureaucratic chain of command by appointing a trusted relative or friend to a special position from which he can demand to see the central bank's private information, or to sideline the bureaucratic chain of command altogether and rely on information from banker cronies. Note, however, that in the last case crony ties to bankers generate incentives for lax regulation; the signaling problem is thus replaced by an incentive problem. This solution can thus be ruled out as a path to stringent regulation.

In democratic environments, the legislature generally serves as a check on the chief executive's power. There is no assurance that it will always allow the chief executive to appoint an official who shares his economic policy preferences to the central bank governorship. For instance, the legislature may refuse to confirm the chief executive's first-choice candidate for the governorship or obstruct the creation of a new ad hoc superbureaucrat position along the lines mentioned above. Such problems are generally absent in authoritarian environments because legislatures, almost by definition, do not serve as a check on the chief executive's power. This means that democracies, unlike authoritarian regimes, cannot credibly commit to always having a solution to the signaling problem. This has the following implications.

Let us consider a best-case scenario for most developing country environments, where the chief executive does not have cronyistic ties to the banking sector and his ideal is a moderately robust banking sector. (Demanding capital levels that exceed solvency requirements is unattractive to politicians because it constrains bank lending, which can depress economic growth.[16]) Recall that we are plausibly defining a moderately stringent regulatory environment as one in which the robustness of the banking sector never falls below a moderate level following the chief executive's response to a default shock. As I show in Chapter 3, even when the chief executive's ideal is a moderately robust banking sector, robustness outcomes have a propensity for sometimes exceeding but also often falling short of a moderate level of robustness in periods when the signaling problem is not solved. Thus, whenever the signaling problem is not solved the outcome is a lax regulatory environment. Because a democracy does not offer a credible assurance that the signaling problem will always be resolved, it embodies an incredible long-term commitment to having

---

[16] A high ratio of capital to assets restricts lending to a low multiple of base capital.

Introduction

Figure 1.2 Ideal points of financial officials and the chief executive.

a stringent regulatory environment. This is the case even when the chief executive has final decision-making power over the level of capital that banks must maintain, and has arm's length (i.e., no personal financial) relationships with bank owners.

The logic when both the finance minister and the central bank governor are signalers is somewhat more complex, but the outcome is the same. I present a simple diagrammatic example below that summarizes the logic of miscommunication when there are two signalers. Let us consider a case where the chief executive's ideal level of banking sector robustness lies between those of the finance minister and the central bank governor, with the ideal point of the former to the left of the chief executive's ideal point. This is purely for illustrative purposes. The theory presented in Chapter 3 allows for the ideal points of these actors to fall elsewhere on the continuum. This case is diagrammatically presented in Figure 1.2.

Let us assume that we start with robustness at the chief executive's ideal level, and that there is then a jump in expected defaults. Let us assume that this jump generates a robustness level at the finance minister's ideal point. These assumptions are also purely for demonstrating the logic in as intuitive a manner as possible. In Chapter 3, I relax both assumptions.

The chief executive does not know the precise level of expected defaults, for the reasons mentioned earlier, and must rely on signals from his advisors. The finance minister would not like the chief executive to respond to the jump in defaults by raising the level of robustness, via capital increases, because robustness is now at his (the finance minister's) ideal level (a capital increase would shift robustness away from his ideal level). He thus has incentives to claim that a jump in expected defaults has not occurred. The central bank governor, on the other hand, would like the chief executive to raise the robustness of the banking sector and bring it closer to his ideal level. Let us suppose that he thus tells the chief executive the true level of expected defaults. The chief executive has to sort out which of the two following scenarios is the true one: 1) Has there really been a jump in expected defaults that justifies a capital increase that would raise robustness? or 2) Has there really not been a jump in expected defaults,

13

and is the central bank governor lying to force a capital increase that would bring robustness closer to his ideal point?

The fact that the chief executive cannot tell which scenario is true means that he is uncertain about whether there has been a jump in expected defaults when he has advisors with preferences that differ from his own, even when one of them is telling the truth. This uncertainty will be present for a far wider range of circumstances than the one described above. Note, for instance, that the finance minister has incentives to deny the central bank governor's claim that a jump in expected defaults has occurred if the jump generates a level of robustness anywhere between his (the finance minister's) and the chief executive's ideal level of robustness. The same arguments can be extended to situations where the disagreement between officials is not about whether a jump has occurred, but rather about the extent of the jump.

The model in Chapter 3 shows that when the preferences of the central bank governor and the finance minister differ from that of the chief executive by a relatively small amount, the chief executive treats the messages from both advisors as being completely uninformative.[17] Given this belief on the part of the chief executive, the governor and the minister lose nothing from disagreeing over every signal, which is completely uninformative, and the vicious circle is once again complete. The chief executive simply ceases to register signals from these officials when the difference between his and their preferences crosses a relatively small threshold.

Let us once again consider the case of a chief executive who does not have incentive problems (i.e., does not have cronyistic ties to the banking sector). The bottom line here is that the uncertainty that results from the signaling strategies makes the chief executive prone to overshooting and undershooting his ideal level of robustness when choosing his regulatory response to default shocks. This means that even a chief executive with a preference for a moderately robust banking sector has a propensity for often falling short of and exceeding his ideal. Because robustness often falls below a moderate level, this amounts to having a lax regulatory environment. Given that democratic environments are not assured of solving the signaling problem for the reasons mentioned earlier, this means that such environments do not embody credible long-term commitments to stringent regulation.

---

[17] A difference of opinion of 4 percentage points with respect to banks' capital buffer is sufficient to make signals completely uninformative.

1.2.2 Absence of Signaling Problems in Authoritarian Environments

In an authoritarian environment the chief executive is likely to have several options to address the signaling problem. Almost by definition, the legislature does not serve as a check to the chief executive's power in an authoritarian environment. Thus the authoritarian chief executive is highly unlikely to be constrained from appointing a friend, a long-trusted associate, or a relative who shares his regulatory preferences to the central bank governorship/finance ministership. I call this the orthodox solution to the signaling problem because it does not entail any institutional innovation. Even if considerations of impressing foreign investors or factional considerations generate incentives for an authoritarian chief executive to appoint officials with preferences different from his own to the above positions, the chief executive has an alternative solution to the signaling problem. Faced with a toothless legislature, he is unlikely to be blocked from appointing a technically skilled relative or a close friend who shares his regulatory preferences to a specially created position from which he can demand confidential information from the governor/finance minister. He could of course also ignore bureaucrats altogether and cultivate banker cronies who provide regulatory advice. (This last option, of course, generates incentive problems, as mentioned earlier.) I call these unorthodox solutions to the signaling problem because they do involve institutional innovation. Either way, the chief executive ensures that regulatory information will be credibly signaled to him at all times. Given the range of options at his disposal, a chief executive in an environment with very few checks can actually credibly promise to always be well informed about defaults.

The implication is as follows. For reasons that I will detail in the next subsection, gridlock is unlikely to be present in environments with very few checks. Keeping in mind the fact that the chief executive in an authoritarian environment is unlikely to be constrained from implementing one of the solutions to the signaling problem, he can credibly commit to always respond to a jump in expected defaults by choosing a sector-wide capital level that is commensurate with keeping banking sector robustness at his ideal level. Where the chief executive has crony ties with bank owners, we should thus expect to see a banking sector that is less than moderately robust after the chief executive responds to the signals being sent to him. His commitment to stringent regulation in this case is thus incredible on account of incentive problems. Where the chief executive has arm's length relations with bank owners, and his preference is thus for a

15

moderately robust banking sector, the same logic should cause us to expect a moderately stringent regulatory environment to be the outcome. Unlike in the case of a democracy, a noncronyistic chief executive of an authoritarian regime can make a credible long-term commitment to stringent regulation.

1.2.3 The Logic of Gridlock

The gridlock-based logic is standard. In democracies, the chief executive often faces institutional barriers to implementing his preferred policies. Approval from the legislature or, where they are present, coalition partners cannot be assured. A failure to adjust bank capital in response to a jump in expected defaults thus cannot be ruled out even when the chief executive would ideally like to have a moderately robust banking sector. For instance, some veto player may object to, and block, the chief executive's decision to close down banks that are technically insolvent. Such a scenario is of course considerably less likely where power is centralized in the chief executive. This means that democratic environments are relatively vulnerable to lax regulation via gridlock, even in the presence of a chief executive who would like to be a stringent regulator.

The same logic can be applied to other aspects of the bank regulatory environment, aside from bank capital, which are described in Appendix 1. For instance, low liquidity, low transparency of regulatory operations (corruption), and low legal protection for regulators from lawsuits filed by banks are considered to be indicators of lax regulation. In an authoritarian environment, a chief executive who is inclined to allow banks to operate with low liquidity, allow regulators to operate in a nontransparent fashion, and provide weak legal support to regulators, thanks to his cronyistic links with bank owners, is unlikely to be prevented from creating a regulatory environment that scores low on stringency in these areas. Likewise, a chief executive facing few checks who has arm's length relations with bank owners should be relatively unconstrained in enforcing high liquidity, forcing regulators to be transparent, and providing strong legal support for bank regulators, and thus creating an environment that scores high on stringency in these areas.

In contrast, in democratic environments chief executives without crony ties to bankers are vulnerable to being blocked by veto players who are opponents of reform, which means that the propensity for lax regulation remains in such political environments.

In sum, the inability of democracies to credibly commit to not having signaling and gridlock problems renders their long-term commitments to stringent regulation incredible. Authoritarian regimes can more credibly commit to not having signaling or gridlock problems. However, this does not mean that all authoritarian environments embody credible commitments to stringent regulation. Where chief executives have cronyistic ties to the banking sector, incentive problems render such commitments incredible. Only authoritarian environments, where the chief executive does not have such ties, can credibly commit to avoiding incentive problems, signaling problems, and gridlock problems. Thus, these are the political environments that are likely to embody credible long-term commitments to stringent bank regulation.

1.3 ALTERNATIVE ARGUMENTS

One analysis that may appear to challenge the above findings is Philip Keefer's. Keefer studies how countries respond to banking crises and finds that fiscal transfers to the financial sector and regulatory forbearance decline in the number of veto players, conditional on the rents that are at stake.[18] Keefer's findings are, however, not comparable with the findings of this book, because the sample selects out countries that have not experienced a banking crisis, in which group stringent regulators are heavily represented.

Aside from the empirical contribution, the technical contribution of this book lies in its identification of incredible signaling as a mechanism leading to lax regulation. By bringing in considerations of signaling, the theory accounts for why several noncronyistic chief executives operating in democratic environments did not even make efforts to persuade other veto players of impending disaster in the banking sector, and the need for stringent regulation. It may be argued that this was because these chief executives knew of the need for tighter regulation but anticipated failure in convincing other veto players, and thus did not act. However, for this explanation to be convincing, we should at least see some evidence that these chief executives knew of the impending disaster. As I show in the case chapters, there is evidence that these chief executives did not know and were also forced to rely on incredible senders of signals. There is also powerful evidence of conflicting signals from advisors. All this

[18] Keefer 2001.

supports the argument that these chief executives were ill informed thanks to signaling problems.

A possible alternative argument that may be made against the institutional- and preference-based perspectives, as well as mine, is that the variations in regulatory environments were the result of variations in bureaucratic capacities rather than variations in political institutions or preferences. Certainly bureaucratic capacity was high for the stringent regulators, Singapore and Hong Kong. However, this was surely endogenous to the preference for stringent regulation of the rulers of these states, because they undertook concerted efforts to build up formidable regulatory bureaucracies. Thus, preferences for stringent regulation cannot be ignored in these environments with very few checks. Furthermore, the very fact that these rulers were able to act on their preferences exclusively in environments with very few checks means that the institutional environment cannot be ignored.

Another possible argument is that variations in regulatory environments may be driven by the degree to which an economy was the recipient of short-term capital flows or "hot money." The implication would be that limits on "hot money" inflows would be associated with the presence of stringent regulatory environments. The problem with such an argument is that short-term debts in Malaysia and the Philippines were indeed low, amounting to 60 percent of foreign reserves in the former and 70 percent of reserves in the latter. However, these countries still failed to establish stringent regulatory environments.

1.4 PLAN FOR THE BOOK AND SUMMARY OF EMPIRICAL CONTRIBUTIONS

In the next chapter, I place the recent concern with bank regulatory governance in the context of the debate over the liberalization of capital flows in the developing world. In Chapter 3, I present the signaling argument. Chapter 4 addresses the democracies of Thailand, South Korea, and the Philippines. The primary empirical contribution here is the spotlight placed for the first time on Chuan Leekpai's, Kim Young Sam's, and Corazon Aquino's failure to find solutions to the signaling problem. Chapters 5 and 6 address the authoritarian countries. The primary empirical contribution in these chapters is the spotlight placed on the diverse solutions to the signaling problem resorted to by authoritarian leaders. Chapter 5 covers the countries that resorted to the unorthodox solution to the signaling problem, namely, Indonesia and Malaysia. Chapter 6 considers the countries that resorted to the orthodox solution, namely, Singapore and Hong Kong. Chapter 7 concludes. Note that in the case study chapters, I only highlight the most egregious departures from stringent regulation in each country. This helps to minimize the technical content of these chapters. Details about other realms of bank regulation are provided in Appendix 1.

2

Bank Regulation in the Debate over Capital Flow Liberalization

In this chapter, I show how a common understanding has emerged that lax bank regulation presents immense dangers for countries operating under liberal capital flows. I begin by presenting the neo-classical case for capital flow liberalization. I then describe the attack on this case following the Asian crisis. Finally, I describe how even prominent proponents of liberalization now accept that the success of liberalization may be contingent on stringent bank regulation.

Prior to the 1980s, most developing countries maintained a significant body of regulations limiting the inflow and outflow of capital across national borders. Foreign exchange transactions had to be approved by government officials and were subject to stringent limits, domestic banks were tightly restrained from borrowing from private sources overseas, and stock markets faced significant legal obstacles to accessing international funds. Starting in the 1980s, the International Monetary Fund (IMF) began to place immense pressure on developing countries to dismantle these and other barriers to the inflow and outflow of international capital. Four arguments, which are sometimes jointly referred to as the neo-classical case for liberalization, were offered in justification for this pressure.

First, it was argued that environments with liberal capital flows, referred to in short as environments with open capital accounts, would help developing countries gain access to funds from developed countries. This would enable them to achieve investment levels that exceeded their domestic savings rates, and thus help them grow faster in the long run.

Second, it was argued that open capital accounts would help countries that were suffering from temporary recessions to engage in short-term countercyclical borrowing from overseas to offset domestic contractions.[1]

---

[1] Obstfeld 1998, 10.

Table 2.1 *GDP Growth Rates*

	1991	1992	1993	1994	1995	1996
Thailand	8.18	8.08	8.38	8.94	8.84	5.52
Philippines	−0.58	0.34	2.12	4.38	4.77	5.76
Malaysia	8.48	7.80	8.35	9.24	9.46	8.58
Indonesia	6.95	6.46	6.50	15.93	8.22	7.98
South Korea	9.13	5.06	5.75	8.58	8.94	7.10
Singapore	7.27	6.29	10.44	10.05	8.75	7.32
Hong Kong	4.97	6.21	6.15	5.51	3.85	5.03

Source: Corsetti et al., 1998.

Third, open capital accounts would allow domestic investors to diversify their portfolios by making international investments. This in turn would make investors less vulnerable to domestic economic shocks, and thus enable them to achieve higher risk adjusted rates of return that would encourage saving and investment.[2]

Finally, the abandonment of controls would help eliminate the "burdensome administrative bureaucracies" that were becoming increasingly ineffective over time thanks to the multiple ways offered by modern financial technology to structure transactions to avoid legal barriers.[3]

In response to these arguments from the IMF, several Asian countries embarked on steps to liberalize capital flows during the 1980s and 1990s. Liberalization was followed by several years of rapid gross domestic product (GDP) growth (Table 2.1).

However, as Table 2.1 shows, the Thai economy had already begun to show signs of slower growth in 1996, and this began to attract the concern of Asian market analysts. As Haggard and MacIntyre (2000) concisely summarize it, "[T]wo issues were of particular concern: the widening current account deficit . . . and unease about overborrowing and mismanagement in the financial sector. The deteriorating current account position reflected a number of factors: sustained real currency appreciation, strongly rising real wages, declining demand in key export markets, and realignment of the yen–dollar relationship. In the financial sector, a very rapid expansion of domestic credit was funded by international borrowing (particularly short-term borrowing). . . . Coupled with this increasingly

[2] IMF Survey 1998, 2.
[3] Eichengreen 1998, 9.

Table 2.2 *Exchange Rates, June 30, 1997, to May 8, 1998*

	Percentage Change 6/30/97–12/31/97	Percentage Change 1/1/98–5/8/98	Cumulative Percentage Change 6/30/97–5/8/98
Thailand	−48.7	−24.7	−36.0
Philippines	−33.9	1.3	−33.0
Malaysia	−35.0	2.1	−33.6
Indonesia	−44.4	−53.0	−73.8
South Korea	−47.7	21.9	−36.2
Singapore	−15.0	4.0	−11.6
Hong Kong	0	0	0

Source: Goldstein 1998, 2.

vulnerable position was a growing perception that banks and finance companies were carrying worrying levels of nonperforming loans and that the country's financial authorities were not overseeing the situation effectively."[4] As rumors began to abound that the Thai exchange rate was no longer sustainable, speculators began a series of attacks on the Thai baht. Finally, on July 2, 1997, Thailand was forced to abandon its fixed exchange rate. This was followed by an exodus of foreign investors from all the Asian economies that had liberalized capital flows, precipitating massive devaluations of several currencies (Table 2.2).

The Asian currency crisis, as Stephan Haggard puts it, "clearly did not fit the profile of the traditional balance of payments crisis... in which monetary and particularly fiscal policy generated unsustainable current account deficits. In none of the most seriously affected countries were budget deficits problematic, and a number of the countries in the region were even in surplus"[5] (Table 2.3).

Since the standard fiscal fundamentals-based explanation did not apply to the Asian crisis, academics quickly became embroiled in a massive debate over the causes for the crisis. One feature that was common to many Asian countries was the fact that they had liberalized capital flows/opened their capital accounts. Responding to this fact, many prominent economists attributed the crisis to the decision to liberalize capital flows and launched an aggressive challenge to the case for capital account liberalization.

---

[4] Haggard and MacIntyre 2001, 61.
[5] Haggard 2000, 5.

Table 2.3 *Fiscal Balance (Percent of GDP)*

	1993	1994	1995	1996
Thailand	1.9	2.7	3.0	0.9
Philippines	−1.5	1.0	0.6	0.3
Malaysia	0.2	2.3	0.9	0.7
Indonesia	−0.4	0.2	−0.2	0.7
South Korea	0.1	0.6	0.5	0.0
Singapore	5.9	7.5	6.1	6.0
Hong Kong	2.1	1.1	−0.3	2.2

Source: Bank Negara 1997a.

Some of the early challenges came from scholars who emphasized the weakness of the case for free capital flows, relative to the case for free trade. In this category of challenges, the prominent trade economist Jagdish Bhagwati argued that the propensity for manias and panics in financial markets rendered the case for free capital flows significantly weaker than that for free trade.[6] In his view, supporters of liberal capital flows "assume that capital mobility is enormously beneficial while simultaneously failing to evaluate its crisis-prone downside. But even a cursory glance at history suggests that such gains may be negligible. After all, China and Japan, different in politics and sociology as well as historical experience, have registered remarkable growth rates without capital account convertibility. Except for Switzerland, capital account liberalization was pretty slow at the outset and did not gain strength till the late 1980s, and some European countries, among them Portugal and Ireland, did not implement it until the early 1990s."[7]

Dani Rodrik argued in a similar vein that, "boom and bust cycles are hardly a side show or a minor blemish in international capital flows; they are the main story."[8] For him, too, this implied that the case for free trade could not be applied to capital flows. Rodrik listed four reasons why financial markets are inherently prone to such boom and bust cycles. First, "asymmetric information combined with implicit insurance results in excessive lending for risky projects."[9] Second, mismatches between short-term liabilities and long-term assets render countries vulnerable to

[6] Bhagwati 1998, 8.
[7] Bhagwati 1998, 10.
[8] Rodrik 1998b, 2.
[9] Rodrik 1998b, 4.

financial panic and bank runs. Third, "when markets cannot observe the intrinsic quality of money managers, these managers are likely to place too little weight on their private information and exhibit herd behavior resulting in excess volatility and contagion effects."[10] Finally, because the prices of financial assets are based on earnings expectations, bubbles can easily emerge and burst, as a consequence of cycles of euphoria and negativity.[11]

Rodrik was especially harsh on his own colleagues in the economics profession for having such a weak understanding of the consequences of liberalizing capital flows. He put it as follows:

A sad commentary of our understanding of what drives capital flows is that every crisis spawns a new generation of economic models. When a new crisis hits, it turns out that the previous generation of models was hardly adequate. Hence, the earliest models of currency crises were based on the incompatibility of monetary and fiscal policies with fixed exchange rates. This seemed to accord well for the myriad balance of payments crises experienced through the 1970s. The debt crisis of 1982 unleashed an entire literature on over-borrowing in developing countries, placing the blame squarely on expansionary fiscal policies (and, in some countries, on inappropriate sequencing of liberalization). But crises did not go away when governments became better behaved on the monetary and fiscal front. For example, the ERM crisis in 1992 could not be blamed on lax monetary and fiscal policies in Europe, and therefore led to a new set of models with multiple equilibria. The peso crisis of 1994–95 did not fit very well either, so economists came up with other explanations – this time focusing on the role of real exchange rate overvaluations and the need for more timely and accurate information on government policies. In the Asian crisis neither the real exchange rate nor inadequate information seems to have played a major role, so attention has shifted to moral hazard and crony capitalism in these countries.[12]

Rodrik concluded his attack on the strategy of capital flow liberalization by conducting an empirical test of the consequences of capital flow liberalization among countries that had unrestricted open capital accounts for at least some time since 1973. His finding was that "capital controls are essentially uncorrelated with long-term economic performance."[13]

Many of the points made by Rodrik were simultaneously made, with varying degrees of emphasis, by other prominent development economists. First, Jeffrey Sachs focused his attention on the consequences of having short-term debt that exceeds foreign reserves under liberal

[10] Rodrik 1998b, 4.
[11] Rodrik 1998b, 4.
[12] Rodrik 1998b, 5–6.
[13] Rodrik 1998b, 9.

capital flows. Applying a model from the banking literature by Diamond and Dybvig, Sachs argued that such a mismatch can generate a phenomenon analogous to a bank run.[14] Consider what happens if some investors panic and want to change the local currency for dollars. Irrespective of the fundamentals, other investors must be concerned that if they are last in line to change their currency, reserves will run out and they will be stuck with a devalued local currency. Thus, it is rational for them to rush to change their local currency for dollars, too, and this precipitates a devaluation that has little to do with fundamentals.

Second, as a consequence of the logic of the Mundell-Fleming hypothesis, countries that open their capital accounts lose the ability to simultaneously target the exchange rate and retain control of the interest rate. Robert Wade and Frank Veneroso pointed out that this is of special significance to countries that have adopted what they call the Asian High Debt Model that is, growth based on high levels of borrowing relative to shareholder equity. In their words, "the risk that an interest rate above the rate of gross profit has disastrous consequences increases with the debt/equity ratio. In higher debt/equity systems firms have to use more of their gross profits on interest charges. A significant rise in interest costs may not be able to be met out of profits, in which case it has to be recapitalized into debt. But the balance sheet may not have room for more debt without threatening the firm's viability."[15] Thus, a high debt–equity ratio sharpens the interest/exchange rate dilemma and generates an exceptionally high risk of a currency collapse under an open capital account.

Finally, Calvo and Mendoza showed that fixed information costs per country can contribute to herd behavior in financial markets that raises the likelihood of a financial collapse under an open capital account.[16] In a similar vein, Scharfstein and Stein showed that, under conditions of asymmetric information, money managers may have incentives to ignore private information. This also contributes to herding effects that can cause excess volatility and severe contagion effects under an open capital account.[17]

The response of proponents of liberalization was twofold. First, Barry Eichengreen argued that Rodrik's result hardly "seals the case against capital account liberalization. Statisticians can fail to find a relationship between capital account liberalization and growth not because none

[14] Radelet and Sachs 1998.
[15] Wade and Veneroso 1998, 8.
[16] Cited in Obstfeld 1998, 26.
[17] Cited in Rodrik 1998b, 4.

exists, but because they have inadvertently omitted from their analysis other variables that are negatively associated with growth but positively associated with the decision to open the capital account. It is plausible that countries that decide to keep their capital accounts open and closed differ from one another in other ways, including ways for which the statistician finds difficult to control."[18]

Second, proponents of liberal capital flows argued that currency and financial crises are by no means an inevitable product of liberal environments. They asserted that lax prudential bank regulation often played a large role in precipitating crises. Thus, stringent regulation could contribute to financial stability, and thus to the likelihood that capital account liberalization is a viable strategy. In this vein, Barry Eichengreen pointed out that "post mortems on the 1992 European and 1995 Mexican crises, while focusing on other factors as the proximate source of financial difficulties, point to the weakness of banking systems as one important reason why governments were unable or unwilling to defend their currencies when they came under attack."[19]

Weaknesses in bank regulation also played an important role in prominent explanations for the 1997 Asian crisis. For Paul Krugman, as well as Michael Dooley, owners of financial institutions who were closely linked to politicians felt that they had an implicit guarantee against failure. This created incentives for heavy lending to speculative projects, largely financed by short-term borrowing from overseas. Regulators' failure to check these tendencies resulted in weak balance sheets.[20] "The fragility of the financial system then prevent[ed] the authorities from mounting a concerted defense of the currency."[21]

Reinforcing claims of a link between banking crises and currency crises under liberal capital flows, Kaminsky and Reinhardt found in an econometric analysis that, since the wave of capital account liberalization in the 1980s, "banking and currency crises [have] become closely entwined...knowing that a banking crisis was under way helps predict a future balance of payments (BOP) crisis."[22] In addition, Frederic Mishkin highlighted the salience of vulnerable banking sectors in rendering currency crises disastrous for developing countries, in contrast

---

[18] Eichengreen 1998, 4.
[19] Eichengreen 1999, 20–21.
[20] Cited in Eichengreen 1999, 20.
[21] Eichengreen 1999, 21.
[22] Kaminsky and Reinhardt 1998.

to developed countries.[23] Mishkin pointed out that, whereas developed countries can actually enjoy high growth after a currency crisis because a lower exchange rate boosts exports, developing countries generally suffer adverse consequences from such an attack. He attributes this difference to the fact that, in developing countries, a currency crisis can have disastrous effects on banking sector balance sheets. Because banks generally carry high levels of foreign debt, a devaluation causes a massive jump in debt obligations. Where banking sectors are weak, which is often the case in the developing world, this chokes off the flow of funds to the domestic economy, including those to exporters. Thus, thanks to difficulties in the banking sector, the consequence of a currency crisis is generally an economic slowdown in developing country contexts.

In light of all the above, proponents of liberal capital flows asserted that stringent prudential bank regulatory governance, as a means of generating robust banking sectors, is "key to financial stability in our modern world."[24] Financial stability under liberal capital flows would, in turn, help render viable the decision to dismantle capital controls.

In sum, thanks in part to the Asian crisis, both sides of the debate are in agreement that incredible long-term commitments to stringent regulation make capital flow liberalization an extremely dangerous proposition. It is thus of immense interest to know which political environments generate incredible commitments to stringent regulation. This is the focus of this book.

---

[23] Mishkin 1996.
[24] Eichengreen 1999, 21.

3

The Signaling Argument

In this chapter, I demonstrate why a small difference in preferences between the chief executive and financial bureaucrats renders signals vague. I also show why the threshold difference in preferences between the chief executive and signalers that generates completely uninformative signals is relatively low in the realm of bank regulation. I begin by defining some terms. I then describe the logic that links a significant difference in preferences between the chief executive and the central bank governor to lax regulation, when the governor is the sole signaler of information collected by bank supervisors. In Section 3.3, I address the scenario in which both the central bank governor and the finance minister are signalers.

3.1 DEFINING SOME TERMS

3.1.1 Banking Sector Robustness

The signaling models presented here focus on a key aspect of a banking sector's robustness: the degree to which a banking sector is capitalized relative to expected loan defaults. I focus on this aspect of robustness for the signaling model because signaling considerations are important in realms where some actors have private information, and this condition is often likely to be met when it comes to the relationship between capitalization and expected defaults, for the reasons listed in Chapter 1.

As per the principles of bank accounting, a bank that has a shareholder capital buffer that is insufficiently large to cover loan defaults is considered to be insolvent. Keeping this in mind, a simple way to assess the robustness of a banking sector is to observe the size of its shareholder capital buffer relative to its expected loan defaults. *Ceteris paribus*, an extremely robust banking sector would be one that has a shareholder capital buffer that is substantially higher than its expected loan defaults. An extremely weak banking sector would be one that has a shareholder capital buffer that is substantially lower than its expected loan defaults. A moderately robust banking sector would be one that falls between these extremes, that is, capital roughly matches expected defaults.

3.1.2 Stringency of the Regulatory Environment

Consider a continuum for banking sector robustness that runs from extremely weak on the left to extremely robust on the right. In the wake of capital flow liberalization, countries are often subjected to substantial exogenous economic shocks that affect the level of expected defaults. A stringent bank regulatory environment would reasonably be one in which the government demands capitalization levels in response to each shock, such that the regulatory response *never* leaves the banking sector below a moderate level of robustness. A lax bank regulatory environment would be one in which the government demands capitalization levels in response to each shock such that the regulatory response does sometimes leave the banking sector below a moderate level of robustness.

I use this measure of stringency because it is consistent with the way the World Bank assesses the bank capital aspect of the regulatory environment. *Ceteris paribus*, the greater the degree to which countries attempt to take account of default risks when imposing capital requirements on banks, the more assured the banking sector is of solvency, and thus the more stringent is the bank regulatory environment.

3.1.3 The Inner Circle of Banking Advisors

I call the set of senior financial officials whose advice the chief executive relies on for assessing robustness the chief executive's *inner circle of banking advisors*. Where there is more than one signaler, the officials who comprise the chief executive's inner circle of banking advisors are generally the minister of finance and the central bank governor. This, of course, refers to the situation when an unorthodox solution to the signaling problem is not resorted to. In the presence of an unorthodox solution, other actors can be included in the inner circle. I exclude subordinates to the central bank governor and the finance minister from the inner circle because they are unlikely to have frequent, unmediated access to the chief executive.

The preferences of these actors over banking sector robustness are captured by the concept of an ideal point. The ideal point in this context refers to the level of robustness that would provide a given actor maximum utility, if it were the policy outcome. The greater the distance of the robustness outcome from the actor's ideal point, the less the utility gained by this actor from the outcome. As far as the preferences of inner circle officials are concerned, they could theoretically have ideal points at any location on the banking sector robustness continuum. Why would an official have an ideal point to the left of the middle, that is, a preference for a weak banking sector? Having a robust banking sector generally requires closing down banks whose expected defaults exceed their shareholder capital base. An official who has close ties to such weak institutions would ideally like to have a banking sector where such institutions are not closed down, but rather are allowed to continue to remain in business despite being undercapitalized. This amounts to saying that such an official would ideally like a weak banking sector, because having a robust banking sector demands closing down weak institutions with which he has close links.

Officials who do not have such close links to weak institutions may be expected to have ideal points at the middle, or to the right of the middle, of the continuum. This is so because such officials are likely to be far more concerned about the consequences to the economy as a whole of having a weak banking sector than about the concerns of owners of weak banks.

3.2 A SCENARIO IN WHICH THE CENTRAL BANK GOVERNOR IS THE SOLE SIGNALER OF INFORMATION COLLECTED BY BANK SUPERVISORS

Consider a game with the following order of moves. In Period 1, the economy is hit by an exogenous shock that generates some proportion of expected loan defaults. This proportion is uniformly distributed over [0,1]. Let us call the realized value of this proportion z. In Period 2, the central bank governor observes z and sends a message to the chief executive about the value of z.[1] (Nothing is lost by substituting the finance

---

[1] The message space is the same as the type space.

minister as the sole signaler in this analysis.) In Period 3, the chief executive observes the message, updates his prior belief about z (that it is uniformly distributed over $[0,1]$), and decides on the proportion of capital to total assets that banks must maintain, which we call k. In Period 4, the outcome level of banking sector robustness, $k - z$, is realized.

The equilibrium concept used here is Perfect Bayesian, in which the receiver (the chief executive) adopts his optimal strategy given his posterior beliefs, the sender (the governor) sends his optimal signal anticipating the receiver's response, and the receiver's beliefs following updating are consistent with the sender's strategy.

Let us make a best-case assumption for most developing country environments that the chief executive's ideal is a moderately robust banking sector, that is, he would like bank capital to equal expected defaults.[2] In other words, the chief executive's optimal response to each z is $k = z$. This would be the same as saying that his ideal point on bank robustness is 0, which is a moderate level of robustness. Let us consider a scenario in which the central bank governor has cronyistic ties to weak banks and would thus like many insolvent banks to remain open. This would be the same as saying that this Central Bank Governor's ideal level of robustness is less than 0, that is, he would like to allow banks that have capital below expected defaults to continue to operate. Let us call the distance between the chief executive's and the governor's ideal points b. The governor's utility is then maximized if $k = z - b$. In effect, the chief executive's payoff function is $-(k - z)^2$ and the central bank governor's payoff function is $-[k - (z - b)]^2$.

To illustrate the intuition of "cheap talk" strategic interaction, I begin with a simple example in which the governor is simply deciding whether to send one signal when expected defaults are high and another when defaults are low, or to simply send one signal that does not discriminate between high and low defaults. The goal of the example is to demonstrate that the precision of communication between the sender and the receiver of signals declines as one moves away from shared preferences. Note that defaults are allowed to rise as high as 1 in this example purely for simplicity of exposition. Later, when I provide substantive content to this example, I restrict the values of defaults to more plausible levels.

---

[2] See Chapter 1 for the rationale for this assumption.

To say that the governor finds it worthwhile to send two different signals for low and high defaults is the same as saying that there is a cut point of defaults between 0 and 1 at which the governor changes from a low defaults signal to a high defaults signal. A cut point at which the governor changes from a low to a high signal must have the characteristic that the governor is indifferent between the two signals when defaults are exactly at that point. To understand how the cut point is established, consider the case when the b parameter, which captures the difference between the chief executive's and the governor's preferences, is .20. Assume for a start that the chief executive's belief (following updating) is that when he gets a signal between 0 and .899, z lies somewhere between these values, and when he gets a signal between .90 and 1, z lies somewhere between these latter values.[3]

When the chief executive gets a signal between 0 and .899, his belief leads him to maximize utility when he chooses a capital level of .45; analogously, when he gets a signal between .90 and 1, he maximizes utility when he chooses a capital level of .95.

Is there a value of z at which the governor is indifferent between low and high default signals? Consider a potential cut point of .90. (In other words, the highest 10% of the defaults distribution is considered to constitute a dangerously high level of defaults.) If the governor sends a low default signal (a message between 0 and .899) when $z = .90$, the chief executive chooses $k = .45$ and the governor's utility is

$$-[k - (z - b)]^2 = -[.45 - (.90 - .20)]^2 = -.0625.$$

If he sends a high signal (a message between .90 and 1), the chief executive chooses .95 and the governor's utility is

$$-[k - (z - b)]^2 = -[(.95) - (.90 - .20)]^2 = -.0625.$$

Thus, at $z = .90$, the governor is indeed indifferent between sending a high and a low signal. In other words, when the distance between the governor's robustness preference and that of the chief executive's is 0.20, there is an incentive for the former to distinguish between high and low default levels by sending different messages for values of z above and below .90. Note that since it is rational for the governor to randomize between 0 and .899 when z lies between these values, and to randomize between .90 and 1 when z lies between these latter values, the chief executive's belief

---

[3] Recall also that z is uniformly distributed.

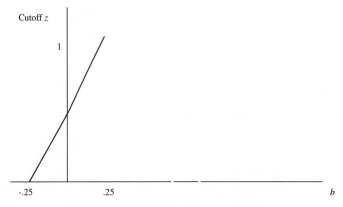

Figure 3.1 Cutoff values for signaling model.

following updating is consistent with the governor's strategy. The final necessary condition for a Perfect Bayesian Equilibrium is also fulfilled.

Consider, however, the consequence of a b of .25. At a z of .90, the governor gets more utility from sending a low signal than a high signal because:

$$-[.45 - (.90 - .25)]^2 = -0.04 > -[(.95 - (.90 - .25)]^2 = -.09.$$

Thus, 0.90 can no longer be the cut point when preferences are so diverse. In fact, when b is .25 or more, it is only at cutoff values of 1 or more that the governor becomes indifferent between signals. When b is $-.25$ or less, it is only at cutoff values of 0 or less that the governor becomes indifferent between signals (see Figure 3.1). This can be verified by experimenting with different cut points and allowing the chief executive's beliefs to be consistent with the strategy.

Because expected defaults lie between 0 and 1, this means that there is a threshold value of b, the preference difference parameter, at which the governor does not send information to the chief executive distinguishing between low and high defaults. The chief executive's belief, consistent with this strategy, is that when he gets any signal of z from the governor, the true value of z could lie anywhere between 0 and 1. He is unable to update his prior belief that z is uniformly distributed in this space. The chief executive thus finds it optimal to choose $k = .5$ at all times, that is, irrespective of the default shock. In effect, once the governor has preferences that are sufficiently far from his own, the chief executive ceases to register any signals regarding default shocks or to respond to them. The consequence, as described in Chapter 1, is that the chief executive has a propensity for often leaving the banking sector short of his ideal level of robustness following shocks, which means that even a preference for a moderate level of robustness is associated with the presence of a lax regulatory environment.

The location of the cut point, as a function of the preference difference parameter, is captured by a simple formula. In this application the formula is simply $x_1 = \frac{1}{2} + 2b$, where x_1 is the cut point between the high and low signals.[4] We can derive this formula simply by setting the utilities to the governor when each message is sent equal to each other, that is, $-[(x_1/2 - (x_1 - b)]^2 = -[(x_1+1)/2 - (x_1 - b)]^2$.

Whenever the absolute value of $b \geq \frac{1}{4}$, x_1 falls outside (0,1). ($b \geq 1/4$ results in $x_1 \geq 1$; $b \leq -1/4$ results in $x_1 \leq 0$.) Thus, whenever the absolute value of $b \geq 1/4$, the central bank governor does not distinguish between low and high defaults in his signals, and his signals are completely uninformative. Thus, the same results hold irrespective of whether the sender has banker cronies or is a hard-line technocrat with a preference for an extremely robust banking sector; the key here is the distance in preferences between sender and receiver rather the direction of the sender's preferences.

The case where the central bank governor only makes a crude distinction between "high" and "low" defaults is one with two intervals, $[0, x_1]$ and $[x_1, 1]$. The case where he does not even make such a crude distinction is one with one interval, $[0,1]$. When the central bank governor makes extremely fine distinctions between all types (default levels) in his signals, there is an infinite number of intervals; this would be a case of perfect communication between the central bank governor and the chief executive. The number of intervals is a function of the preference difference parameter and is the largest integer below:[5]

$$\tfrac{1}{2}[1 + \sqrt{1 + 2/|b|}].$$

This formula indicates that when $b = 0$, there is an infinite number of intervals. In other words, when the chief executive and the governor have identical preferences, there is perfect communication between them. The chief executive is thus invulnerable to lax regulation on account of problems with credible communication. This is what is achieved when

---

[4] See Gibbons 1992. The difference in sign from Gibbons' original formulation, which is based on Crawford and Sobel 1982, is that I use a slightly different payoff function.
[5] See Gibbons 1992 and Crawford and Sobel 1982.

either the orthodox or unorthodox solution to the signaling problem is implemented.

Note, however, that when $b > 0$, we have less than an infinite number of intervals. In other words, there is vagueness in communication that generates a propensity for the chief executive to miscalculate his response to default shocks. This is the signaling problem that was described in Chapter 1.

Note also that this formula indicates that whenever the absolute value of $b \geq \frac{1}{4}$, there is only one interval. (For instance, when $b = 1/4$, the above formula equals 2 and the largest integer below 2 is 1.) In other words, whenever the absolute value of $b \geq \frac{1}{4}$, the central bank governor is not communicating any useful information to the chief executive. (In technical terms, the central bank governor simply randomizes across the entire type space in his messages, which is completely uninformative.) Under such circumstances the chief executive simply ignores the central bank governor.

In the analysis above, loan defaults were assumed to be uniformly distributed over [0,1] for simplicity of exposition. This, however, is clearly not a realistic assumption and needs to be modified if we want to know the true value of b at which communication becomes completely uninformative. The assumption is not realistic for the simple reason that even after a crisis as catastrophic as the Asian crisis, the highest level of peak nonperforming loans in a country was 50 percent.[6] Nonperforming loans, in J. P. Morgan's definition, are loans on which no payments have been made for 3 months. This is an upper bound indicator of loan defaults, because some loans may return to repayment status and may not be written off. Even this figure, achieved by Thailand, was an extreme outlier. Countries like Korea and Malaysia that also experienced extreme currency crises had peak nonperforming loans of 25 percent following the crisis.[7] Thus, for the real world even an upper bound of .50 would make for an extremely conservative assumption of the range of defaults.

We also need to take account of the fact that nonperforming loans exceeding 15 percent sector-wide are generally only seen in the wake of catastrophic crises like the Asian crisis. (No country considered here had a nonperforming loan ratio exceeding 15% prior to the currency turmoil.[8]) In other words, except in the wake of catastrophic currency

---

[6] J.P. Morgan Asian Financial Markets, Second Quarter 1999, 38.
[7] J.P. Morgan Asian Financial Markets, Second Quarter 1999, 38.
[8] See Corsetti et al. 1998.

crises, the probability of observing defaults significantly exceeding .15 is effectively very close to 0. Because I am considering the years prior to 1997, it appears reasonable to assume that, for all practical purposes, defaults are uniformly distributed over [0, .15]. This assumption is also appealing because it leaves an uninformed chief executive always choosing a capital ratio that is reasonable by developing country standards (a little less than 8%), which is not the case when the upper bound is raised.[9]

The implication of using .15 as the upper bound is simply that the threshold value of b at which no communication occurs now becomes 15% of .25 = .0375. This can be readily observed in the two interval case as follows. Set the utility to the governor from the two messages equal to each other, that is, $-[(x_1/2 - (x_1 - b)]^2 = -[(x_1 + .15)/2 - (x_1 - b)]^2$. This yields a cut point as a function of b of $x_1 = .15/2 + 2b$. At values of $b \geq .0375$, $x_1 \geq .15$, and thus the governor no longer distinguishes between high and low defaults in his signals when b meets this low threshold.

The implications for bank regulation are significant. As long as the chief executive is forced to operate with a governor who would like to maintain a capital buffer over expected defaults that is approximately 4 percentage points more or less than he (the chief executive) would ideally like, there will be *no* useful communication between the governor and the chief executive. As described in detail in Chapter 1, the consequence, in the absence of a solution to the signaling problem, is a failure on the part of the chief executive to register default shocks, which leads to lax regulation.

A difference of 4 percentage points is well within the bounds of what one observes in policy debates between politicians and financial bureaucrats. For instance, as the Indonesian case study shows, the central bank governor wanted banks to maintain a capital asset ratio of 8 percent,

---

[9] The implications of raising the upper bound above .15 are straightforward. The threshold difference in preferences at which there is no communication rises proportionately with an increase in the upper bound. Thus, assuming that the upper bound is .50 instead of .15 raises the threshold to .125. However, aside from assigning high probability values to what are, in fact, low probability events (which is what defaults >.15 are), this upper bound is entirely unreasonable because it calls for an uninformed Chief Executive to always choose an extremely high capital ratio of 25%, which is unheard of in the developing world. All upper bounds that are significantly above .15 have the same undesirable properties of assigning overly high probabilities to low probability events, and of having the uninformed Chief Executive adhere to unreasonably high capital ratios at all times.

while imposing strict limits on bank owners making substantial loans to themselves. (If bank owners make loans to themselves in excess of the capital they have put in, this amounts to a negative capital asset ratio.) In contrast, President Soeharto was quite content with allowing bank owners to make massive loans, well in excess of capital, to themselves. This case was thus one with a difference in preferences of well over 4 percentage points, perhaps even 8 percent. Indeed, as the theory predicts, the evidence is that Soeharto did not rely on his central bank governor as a signaler and instead resorted to getting signals from cronies in the banking sector who shared his preferences (i.e., an unorthodox solution to the signaling problem).

3.3 A SCENARIO IN WHICH BOTH THE FINANCE MINISTER AND THE CENTRAL BANK GOVERNOR ARE SIGNALERS OF INFORMATION COLLECTED BY BANK SUPERVISORS

The goal of this section is to show that the substantive conclusion of the previous section holds true when the analysis is expanded to multiple signalers.

3.3.1 A Sketch of the Causal Mechanism for a Model with Two Signalers

Let us call an advisor with an ideal point that is far left of the middle of the robustness continuum Official L and an advisor with an ideal point far right of the middle of the continuum Official R. As a benchmark case, let us assume that the inner circle consists of the chief executive, Official L, and Official R. (It makes no difference if it is the central bank governor or the finance minister who takes the L or the R position.) In this benchmark case, the chief executive's ideal point is assumed to be at a moderate level of robustness, that is, at the middle of the robustness continuum. In the benchmark case, I also assume that the chief executive makes the final decision on the degree to which banks must be capitalized, unconstrained by other actors. We have now effectively constructed a benchmark inner circle in which inner circle advisors have preferences that are extremely distant from the chief executive and each other, and a benchmark decision-making environment where the chief executive is not obstructed from choosing the degree to which banks must be capitalized by bargaining deadlocks with other veto players. I first formally evaluate the consequences of having such conditions in place and subsequently evaluate the consequences of altering these benchmark conditions.

Consider a scenario in which, due to an exogenous economic shock, banks end up with significant quantities of loans that are likely to go into default in the near future. In the absence of any regulatory response from the government, such as insisting that banks increase the shareholder capital that they keep on hand as a buffer against anticipated loan defaults, this would leave the banking sector far left of the middle of the robustness continuum.

Consider a game in which the central bank governor and the finance minister have private information of the value of expected defaults, gleaned from bank supervisors' examinations of banks' accounts. The chief executive does not have the technical skills to decipher banks' accounts and thus cannot arrive at an independent assessment. (The chief executive knows the ideal points of inner circle members, and the only informational asymmetry in the game relates to expected defaults.) The central bank governor and the finance minister each sends a signal of the value of expected defaults to the chief executive. Recall that we are considering a benchmark environment where the inner circle advisors are Official L and Official R. Because neither advisor shares the chief executive's ideal point, the latter cannot automatically believe either of the advisors' signals. (The advisors would prefer robustness outcomes at their own ideal points rather than at the chief executive's ideal point and are thus not assured of telling the truth.) The chief executive attempts to infer the true level of expected defaults and then decides on the appropriate capital buffer level with the goal of ending up with a banking sector that is at his ideal level of robustness. (Robustness = shareholder capital buffer/total loans − expected defaults/total loans.) Official R has incentives to inform the chief executive that expected defaults are extremely high, because a weak banking sector causes him immense disutility. However, Official L has very different incentives due to the fact that his ideal point is far left of the center of the robustness continuum. As long as the robustness outcome when the chief executive is uncertain of the true level of potential defaults is closer to Official L's ideal point than to a moderate level of robustness, this official will have incentives to generate uncertainty by contradicting Official R's signal when the expected default level is high.

Contradictory signals from the two advisors generate uncertainty for the chief executive as to whether the expected default level is truly as high as Official R claims, or if Official R is exaggerating the problem to generate a robustness outcome that is at his (Official R's) own ideal point, which is to the right of the chief executive's own ideal point. The consequence of this uncertainty is that the chief executive often underestimates or overestimates the level of expected defaults. Underestimates result in a failure to tighten capital buffer regulations adequately to create a moderately robust banking sector, while overestimates have the opposite consequence. The fact that underestimates often occur means that countries where the chief executive is forced to operate with inner circle advisors with polarized preferences are vulnerable to ending up with lax regulatory environments. This is the case even under the assumptions that the chief executive's ideal point is a moderately robust banking sector and there are no bargaining deadlocks.

Identical to the single-signaler scenario, once the preferences of both signalers reach a threshold distance from that of the chief executive, the signals become completely uninformative. (For every value of defaults there are contradictory signals.) For the same reasons as those given in the single-signaler scenario, the chief executive then becomes vulnerable to failing to register default shocks altogether, and thus failing to respond to them. The model below shows that the threshold in the multiple-signaler case also lies at a 4 percentage difference in ideal points, with respect to the capital buffer over expected defaults.

The results are unchanged if both advisors have preferences to the left or to the right of the chief executive's ideal point. As long as the advisor with the ideal point that is closest to the chief executive's has an ideal point that is 4 percentage points away from the chief executive's ideal point, the signals will be uninformative and the chief executive is vulnerable to failing to register shocks altogether.

This outcome is in sharp contrast to what we should expect in an inner circle where the preferences of the inner circle advisors converge on the chief executive's ideal point. Because they share the chief executive's ideal point, inner circle advisors have incentives to truthfully signal the chief executive that the level of expected defaults is high when it is so. This is the case because, if the chief executive remains uncertain and thus adequate countervailing regulatory action is not taken, the robustness outcome is worse for these advisors than if the chief executive is informed, and chooses a capital buffer level that brings the banking sector to his and their mutual ideal point. Knowing that his inner circle advisors share his ideal point, the chief executive will believe these officials' matching, true signals and will immediately respond by choosing capital buffer regulations commensurate with bringing the banking sector to his and their ideal level. Thus, we should generally **not** expect to see communication problems between advisors and the chief executive generate robustness outcomes that differ from the chief executive's ideal point in countries with such inner circles. (As I demonstrate in Section 3.3, the above outcome is also likely to occur if the chief executive can appoint one inner circle member who shares his ideal point.)

The above analysis suggests that when the chief executive and his advisors are unpolarized in their preferences, the robustness outcome will vary according to the chief executive's ideal point. (This assumes that the chief executive has mechanisms in place to address agency problems, which is plausible especially because a chief executive should be unobstructed from firing "slacker" officials in the centralized environments where such inner circles should be expected.) Thus, as long as the chief executive at least has a moderately robust banking sector as his ideal, a country with an unpolarized inner circle is likely to have a stringent regulatory environment.

Recall that the chief executive has a propensity to miscalculate the appropriate regulatory response where the inner circle is polarized. To have a stringent regulatory environment in the presence of such an inner circle, these miscalculations must not result in banking sectors that are less than moderately robust. I formally demonstrate in the next section that the chief executive has to have an ideal point that is implausibly far to the right of the middle of the robustness continuum to have a stringent regulatory environment under such conditions. The threshold ideal point for stringent regulation declines as the inner circle becomes less and less polarized.

3.3.2 Preliminary Assumptions

The key results presented here build on seminal work on costless signaling or "cheap talk" models by Crawford and Sobel (1982), Austen-Smith (1987), and Gilligan and Krehbiel (1987, 1989). The banking sector figures in my argument in the following way. Defaults are not in a bank's interest. Banks thus exert efforts to minimize these defaults. However, an environment with liberal capital flows exposes banks' loan portfolios to random exogenous shocks. Since expected defaults are subject to random chance up to a point under such circumstances, I conceive of expected defaults as a random variable, which I label ω. I assume that ω is uniformly distributed with mean $\bar{\omega}$. ω is assumed to be in $[0, .15]$ for the same reasons listed in the single-signaler scenario.

3.3.3 The Players

There are three strategic players in this game: the chief executive, the finance minister, and the central bank governor. The banking sector, because it consists of a large number of highly fragmented institutions that would tend to have coordination problems, is not considered to be a strategic player. The chief executive is labeled c. Whoever of the finance minister or the central bank governor has preferences closer to the right end of the banking sector robustness continuum is labeled s_1 while the one who has preferences closer to the left end of the continuum is labeled s_2. (s refers here to the fact that these two actors are *senders* of signals.)

3.3.4 Information Structure and the Order of Moves

The goal of this model is to demonstrate the consequences of having inner circle advisors with ideal points far away from/close to the chief executive's ideal point. As far as the causes are concerned, however, recall the discussion in Chapter 1 about the constraints faced by democratic leaders against implementing the orthodox and unorthodox solutions to the signaling problem.

Period 1 covers the years immediately following capital flow liberalization. In Period 1, shocks to the banking sector's loan portfolio generate a realized value of ω, which I call z. The central bank governor and finance minister accurately infer z from financial statistics collected by bank supervisors. The chief executive, not having the requisite training, cannot interpret these statistics and does not know z. All he knows about z in this period is his prior belief that ω is uniformly distributed in $[0, 0.15]$. Every aspect of this game, aside from z, is commonly known to all the strategic players.

In Period 2, the central bank governor and the finance minister simultaneously send individual messages (signals) of the value of z, labeled m_1 and m_2, to the chief executive. m_1 is the signal sent by s_1 while m_2 is the signal sent by s_2.

41

In Period 3, the chief executive observes the messages and updates his prior belief about the value of z using Bayes' rule. I denote the posterior belief $g(z; m_1, m_2)$.

In Period 4, the chief executive decides on the percentage of the value of total loans that capital injected by bank shareholders must constitute.[10] This percentage is labeled k. In the benchmark case, the chief executive is unconstrained in his choice of k.

In Period 5, the chief executive's decision yields a policy outcome with respect to banking sector robustness, x, which refers to capital injected by shareholders as a percentage of total loans, net of expected defaults as a percentage of total loans. Thus, $x = k - z$.

3.3.5 Utility Functions

Each player is assumed to have a quadratic utility loss function in banking sector robustness outcomes, x, which are points in a unidimensional space.[11] x_{s1}, x_{s2}, and x_c are the ideal levels of robustness of Sender 1, Sender 2, and the chief executive, respectively. The utility functions of the actors are then, respectively:

$$u_{s1} = -(x_{s1} - x)^2, \qquad u_{s2} = -(x_{s2} - x)^2, \qquad \text{and} \qquad u_c = -(x_c - x)^2.$$

3.3.6 Location of Ideal Points

Recall that a banking sector for which x is less than 0 is weak, and a banking sector for which x is significantly greater than 0 is extremely robust. A banking sector that has just about enough capital to cover expected defaults is an intermediate case, a moderately robust banking sector. Recall also that we are first considering the benchmark case where the chief executive's ideal is a moderately robust banking sector. Thus, $x_c = 0$. In the benchmark case, the advisors in the inner circle are Official R and Official L, who have ideal points on either side of the chief executive. Thus $x_{s1} > 0$ and $x_{s2} < 0$. I relax this assumption in the comparative statics. I initially assume that $x_{s2} = -x_{s1}$. This allows us to use the level

---

[10] The chief executive's goal is to end up with an outcome, x, that is at his ideal point.

[11] Technically x can take any value between -1 and 1. However, as will become apparent, we are concerned with a much narrower range of outcomes for the application at hand.

of x_{s1} as the indicator of polarization. I also relax this assumption in the comparative statics.

3.3.7 Equilibrium Concept

The equilibrium concept used here is Perfect Bayesian. For a proposed equilibrium to qualify as a Perfect Bayesian equilibrium, four conditions must be met: s_1's signaling strategy must maximize his expected utility given s_2's optimal signaling strategy and the chief executive's optimal choice of k; s_2's signaling strategy must maximize his expected utility given s_1's optimal signaling strategy and the chief executive's optimal choice of k; the chief executive's choice of k must maximize his expected utility given his posterior belief about the value of z; and the chief executive's posterior belief must be consistent with the optimal strategies of the senders as per Bayes' rule.

3.3.8 Proposition

Building on the path-breaking work of Crawford and Sobel, Gilligan and Krehbiel prove the existence of an equilibrium that, in the form that is appropriate for this application, has the following characteristics.[12] I first describe this equilibrium and then conduct my own comparative statics (changes from benchmark conditions).

Proposition: There exists a Perfect Bayesian Equilibrium with the following characteristics:

a. When z takes values greater than $\varpi + 2x_{s1}$ or less than $\varpi - 2x_{s1}$, the two senders signal the true value of z to the chief executive. The chief executive chooses $k = z$ and the robustness outcome is $x = 0$.

b. When z takes values between $\varpi - 2x_{s1}$ and $\varpi + 2x_{s1}$, the two senders send conflicting signals of the value of z. The chief executive chooses $k = \varpi$ and the robustness outcome is $x = \varpi - z$.

A detailed verbal description of the intuition underlying this equilibrium is in Appendix 2, and the formal proof is in Appendix 3.

---

[12] Crawford and Sobel 1982 and Gilligan and Krehbiel 1989.

3.3.9 Comparative Statics (Changes from Benchmark Conditions)

3.3.9.1 The Impact of Changes in Polarization (x_{s1}). Recall that ω is a uniformly distributed random variable in $[0, .15]$. Because ω is uniformly distributed in $[0, .15]$, $\varpi = .075$. It follows that when $x_{s1} = .0375$, $\varpi + 2x_{s1} = .15$ and $\varpi - 2x_{s1} = 0$. Thus, for $x_{s1} \geq .0375$, the chief executive receives conflicting signals of the level of z for its entire range of values.

A value of x_{s1} that is substantially greater than .0375 is entirely plausible. One indication of this is that the Bank for International Settlements, which is staffed by technocrats, has long been recommending that banks should maintain a ratio of capital to risk weighted assets of 8 percent, after deducting expected defaults from capital. Likewise, it is entirely plausible for an official with close ties to extremely weak banks to ideally want the government to tolerate shareholder capital levels that fall short of expected defaults by .0375. This would allow banks with which he has ties to remain in operation.

The implications for banking sector robustness are as follows. Consider what happens in countries where $x_{s1} \geq .0375$ if, in the wake of capital flow liberalization, z is higher than ϖ. Since $\varpi + 2x_{s1} \geq .15$, the chief executive, receiving conflicting signals, will choose $k = \varpi$ for all realizations of z. Because $x = k - z$, any incidence of z that is higher than ϖ in the wake of capital flow liberalization will result in a realization of x that is less than 0, which amounts to a weak banking sector. Then, given a uniform distribution of ω, a weak banking sector has a 50 percent probability of occurring, and the propensity for having a weak banking sector following the government's regulatory response is high in such environments. As per our earlier definition, this is consistent with having a lax bank regulatory environment.

As x_{s1} decreases below .0375, $\varpi + 2x_{s1}$ decreases and $\varpi - 2x_{s1}$ increases. Because the chief executive will now receive matching, true signals of more values of z, the number of z realizations for which the chief executive will choose $k < z$ goes down. Thus, as the inner circle becomes less polarized, the likelihood of having a weak banking sector following the government's regulatory response goes down. (In other words, the bank regulatory environment becomes less lax as x_{s1} decreases below .0375.) When $x_{s1} = 0$, the chief executive is always perfectly informed of the value of z and thus always chooses $k = z$, which means that the robustness of the banking sector never falls below the chief executive's ideal point. Under such conditions bank regulation is stringent.

If we relax the assumption that $x_{s2} = -x_{s1}$, it is possible to have an unproblematic signaling environment even if one of these ideal points is far away from 0. This would be the case when the chief executive can appoint either a central bank governor or a finance minister whose ideal point matches his own and can thus effectively ignore the other advisor's signals. An unproblematic signaling environment would also be the outcome if the chief executive is free to break the bureaucratic chain of command to appoint a trusted associate (one who shares his ideal point) to observe bank regulatory information along with the central bank governor and the finance minister. In such a case, the chief executive can simply ignore the latter two actors and be perfectly informed. Thus, the propensity for lax regulation in the absence of gridlock is limited to situations where both the central bank governor and the finance minister have preferences that differ from those of the chief executive's, and the chief executive is not free to break the bureaucratic chain of command by appointing a trusted associate as a third signaler.

3.3.9.2 Comparative Statics on x_c. As described in Chapter 1, the likelihood that there is no signaler who shares the chief executive's ideal point is extremely low in authoritarian environments. This means that it is sufficient for $x_c = 0$, that is, for the chief executive to have a moderately robust banking sector as his ideal, for an authoritarian political environment to have a stringent regulatory environment. As far as the comparative statics are concerned, when $x_c \geq 0$ in an authoritarian environment, the outcome will be a stringent regulatory environment. (Recall that the outcome is at the chief executive's ideal point.) When $x_c < 0$, the outcome is a lax regulatory environment.

A democratic environment, however, retains a propensity for generating inner circles in which the advisors and the chief executive have significantly different preferences from each other. Given this propensity, how far does x_c have to increase above 0 to be assured of getting a stringent regulatory environment? Recall that in the benchmark case the chief executive chooses $k = \varpi = .075$ when he receives conflicting signals. He does so because this choice maximizes his expected utility on receiving conflicting signals, by generating an expected value of $x = 0$, which is his ideal point. (The expected value of $z = \varpi$ is .075. Thus, given that $x = k - z$, the expected value of x when he chooses $k = .075$ is 0.)

However, as described earlier, when the chief executive chooses $k = \varpi = .075$, he ends up getting $z > k$, and thus $x < 0$, often. To get a stringent environment, the chief executive's choice of k must be sufficiently high that z is never greater than k. (This simply follows from our definition of a stringent regulatory environment.) To meet this goal, the chief executive must choose $k = .15$ when signals conflict with each other.

The fact that a rational chief executive must choose k with the goal of getting an expected value of x that matches his ideal point when getting conflicting signals implies the following. Because $k-$(the expected value of z) must equal his ideal point, and because the expected value of $z = .075$ when conflicting signals are received, a rational chief executive who chooses $k = .15$ must have $x_c = .15 - .075 = .075$.[13] Such an ideal point, as may be recalled, is comparable to the ideal point of a technocrat at the Bank for International Settlements, which is implausible for a chief executive facing checks and balances against behaving like an apolitical technocrat.

In sum, under all plausible sets of preference conditions for the chief executive, that is, for all x_c not too far from 0, democratic countries continue to embody a propensity for lax prudential bank regulation even after we assume away bargaining gridlocks. This is so because such environments retain a propensity for having a central bank governor and a finance minister with ideal points that are far from the chief executive's ideal point.

All of the above comparative statics were conducted with the benchmark assumption that the chief executive is unconstrained from choosing k with a view to getting a value of x that matches his ideal point. I conclude by addressing the impact of adding constraints on the choice of k.

The following analysis is contingent on there being at least one veto player whose ideal point is at a lower level of robustness than the chief executive. (If there is no such veto player, the prospects for weak regulation are no worse than under the last comparative statics exercises.) Suppose we add the following constraint to the benchmark case: The chief executive is prevented by veto players with ideal points to the left of his own from choosing a k that is high enough to generate his ideal point as the expected outcome. (In other words, he is forced to choose $k < \varpi$.) The consequence is that the incidence of $k < z$ will increase. This is the same as saying that outcomes below $x = 0$ will occur even more frequently, resulting in an even laxer bank regulatory environment.

---

[13] Recall that conflicting signals are received when z lies between $\varpi - 2x_{s1}$ and $\varpi + 2x_{s1}$.

To sum up, even if the chief executive in a democratic environment faces an implausibly low level of impediments on regulatory decision making from other veto players, such an environment remains vulnerable to lax regulation under all plausible assumptions for the chief executive's preferences. However, there are plausible conditions, namely, a preference for a moderately robust banking sector on the part of the chief executive, under which an authoritarian country does not have a propensity for having a lax regulatory environment.

4

Incredible Signaling in Democracies
The Cases of Thailand, South Korea, and the Philippines

In this chapter, I address the three countries in the sample that were democracies. At some point in time each of these countries had a chief executive without crony links to bankers, who was forced to operate with a signaler/signalers with regulatory preferences that were different from his own thanks to the checks on his power. On each occasion there is evidence of serious problems in communication that went unresolved, resulting in lax regulation. This, of course, is in line with the predictions of the theory.

4.1 THAILAND

Thailand proved to be an extremely lax regulator of banks in the wake of capital flow liberalization in the early 1990s. Prior to liberalization, however, Thailand's central bank was not considered to be an extremely lax regulator. To place Thailand's post-liberalization regulatory performance in context, I begin with a background section that addresses the political determinants of bank regulation in Thailand from the 1960s to liberalization. In Section 4.2, I describe the political environment in which Chuan Leekpai, the Thai prime minister for the three years following capital flow liberalization, operated. In Section 4.3, I describe Chuan's inner circle of banking advisors. In Section 4.4, I describe Thailand's weak record of enforcing bank regulations during Chuan's term, and Section 4.5 addresses the regulatory performance of Chuan's successors.

4.1.1 Background: Bank Regulatory Governance
in Thailand Before 1992

In the three decades prior to the liberalization of capital flows in 1992–93, Thailand was predominantly governed by a succession of authoritarian or semi-authoritarian regimes, that is, regimes with very few checks on the chief executive's power. The lion's share of political power in all these nondemocratic regimes rested with the military. Important institutional changes in 1958 laid the groundwork for bank regulation in subsequent decades. In this year, General Sarit Thanarat, who had just taken power in a coup, embarked on a series of reforms aimed at delegating significant aspects of financial decision making to technocrats. He did so for three reasons.

First, ethnic-Chinese industrialists, who were key supporters of Sarit's coup, were in favor of a departure from the loose macroeconomic policies of the earlier regime.[1] Furthermore, based on the experiences of neighboring countries, many members of the military were adherents of the notion that weak macroeconomic governance would generate crises that would provide foreign governments with immense powers over government policies, tantamount to de facto colonization.[2] Over and above these concerns, Sarit needed to send a strong signal of future good governance to attract development funds from international financial institutions.[3] The creation of a strong financial technocracy offered the promise of satisfying the desires of domestic groups as well as the international financial institutions. Sarit thus created a nucleus of four financial institutions that would be left to technocrats to run in a conservative fashion. Included among these institutions was the central bank, which, in addition to controlling monetary policy, was also responsible for bank regulation.[4]

As far as the central bank is concerned, Sarit's first major action was to appoint as governor a highly respected bureaucrat, Puey Ungphakorn. Puey (1959–71) adopted a systematic plan to build a highly skilled, apolitical, and honest cadre of bureaucrats at the central bank. Thailand's best students were encouraged to join this institution. New recruits were then sent on central bank scholarships to Europe and the United States to be indoctrinated in the neo-classical principles espoused by Puey.[5]

Puey's plan was dramatically successful. It became common for not only the best students, but also for skilled members of the aristocracy

---

[1] Christensen et al. 1997, 26.

[2] Doner and Unger in Haggard, Lee, and Maxfield 1993, 97. Thailand is one of the few developing countries that has never been colonized.

[3] Maxfield 1997, 78.

[4] The four bodies were the Bank of Thailand (the central bank), the National Economic Development Board, the Bureau of the Budget, and the Ministry of Finance. Ammar 1997, 7.

[5] Bank of Thailand 1992, 131.

and the royal family to join the ranks of financial technocrats, known as *karatchakan* (servants of the crown).[6] With the constant infusion of "the best and the brightest," the central bank quickly became an organization that fulfilled the military's preference for macroeconomic stability.

Thailand's macroeconomic performance in the 1960s, 1970s, and, to some degree, the 1980s was exceptional. Monetary policy was conducted in an exceedingly conservative fashion, alongside an impressive record on the part of fiscal technocrats in maintaining balanced budgets. Inflation rates were kept to less than 5 percent, which meant that the *baht* was only devalued twice in the decade and a half prior to capital account liberalization.

Thanks to the high degree of macroeconomic stability, the Thai government was able to successfully engineer a transition from a strategy of import substitution to one based on manufactured exports. As Christensen et al. put it, "the Thai government has been most effective in maintaining a macroeconomic equilibrium conducive to trade, investment, and the growth of private firms."[7] Under the institutional arrangements described above, Thailand became one of the fastest growing economies in the world, with annual GDP growth rates of close to 7 percent.[8]

It should be emphasized that, outside of the four agencies mentioned above, conditions were far more akin to those seen in other parts of the developing world. As Christensen et al. concisely describe it, "sectoral policies did not undergo extensive reform and as previously they were not guided by a clear or coherent development philosophy ... patronage continued to influence important decisions in the line ministries."[9] In other words, sound microeconomic governance was less of a priority to the military than sound macroeconomic governance. However, bank regulation was protected by the military from outright cronyism to a greater degree than realms of microeconomic policy that fell under the purview of line ministries because, by widespread tradition, it fell under the purview of the central bank. Thailand's track record of bank regulation under military rule is consistent with the central bank's somewhat protected status.

It was Puey who was responsible for establishing the legislative foundation for bank regulation in Thailand, by pushing through the Commercial

---

[6] *Asiamoney* February 1997, 16.
[7] Christensen et al. 1997, 23.
[8] Ammar and Sobokchai 1998, 1.
[9] Christensen et al. 1997, 27.

Banking Act in 1962. This Act broke new ground in the prudential regulatory realm by giving the Bank of Thailand substantial powers to regulate commercial banks' reserve requirements, cash reserves, credit extensions, and branch openings, besides granting greater powers to inspect bank accounts and to gain control of a bank.[10] Puey's successors were reasonably prompt in averting excessive strain to the banking sector by tightening regulation beyond the levels specified in the 1962 Act.

The first such instance occurred in the late 1970s. The Thai banking sector had long consisted of sixteen commercial banks. In response to tight controls on the expansion of the number of commercial banks, many finance companies began to emerge in the 1970s that were operating as de facto banks.[11] The number of such companies had grown from 17 in 1971 to 113 by the late 1970s. Not being subject to the strictures of the Commercial Banking Act, many of these companies engaged in risky lending practices and became insolvent in 1978. At this point, it became apparent to central bank officials that the pre-existing regulatory framework, as represented by the Commercial Banking Act, did not adequately take account of the similarity between Thai finance companies and banks, or provide the central bank with sufficient regulatory decision-making powers to ensure the stability of financial intermediation. The central bank thus successfully pressed for tighter laws for licensing and regulating finance companies. This effort came to fruition with a new Act on the Undertaking of Finance Business, Securities Business, and Credit Foncier Business in 1979. (Henceforth, following convention, I include finance companies as being part of the Thai banking sector.[12])

When, in the face of a sustained recession and high interest rates in the early 1980s, several finance companies teetered on the edge of bankruptcy once again, the central bank realized that the new Act was insufficiently stringent for the exigencies of the times. This law was thus amended twice, in 1983 and in 1985, as a means of tightening the regulation of finance companies.

In addition to these legal measures, the central bank organized a consortium of all the commercial banks to create a 5 billion *baht* Fund for

---

[10] Bank of Thailand 1992, 177.

[11] Finance companies in the Thai context are *de facto* banks because their liabilities only differ marginally from short-term bank deposits. (Thai finance companies raise funds through fixed time promissory notes. However, the notes can be withdrawn on demand which means that these notes are, for all practical purposes, short-term deposits.) See Johnston 1991, 243.

[12] See previous footnote for the reason why this convention is justified.

Supplementing the Liquidity of Financial Institutions. This fund was used to provide fully collateralized liquidity support for finance companies unaffiliated with commercial banks. To qualify for longer term assistance, finance companies were required to increase their capital levels as well as their operational efficiency, after writing off their accumulated losses from the value of capital.[13] Twenty-four finance and security companies were closed down altogether as a means of enhancing the robustness of the banking sector.[14]

The regulatory reforms introduced in the 1980s went beyond measures relating to finance companies. In 1985, the central bank replaced the old Commercial Banking Act with a new one that substantially increased its powers of oversight. This expansion of powers was put to good use when three commercial banks approached insolvency in the midst of a deep recession in the mid-1980s. In the case of one bank, the Asia Trust Bank, the central bank replaced the management and merged the bank into the state-owned Krung Thai Bank.[15] In the case of two banks, the central bank forced shareholders to write off their losses and inject new equity.[16] In addition, all banks were asked to increase their capital buffer to safeguard themselves from potential defaults. Limited low-interest loans were provided under strict conditions only to banks that "were cooperative and willing to put up more capital."[17] In sum, consistent with the military's preference for insulating the central bank to some degree from cronyistic influences, the Thai central bank was not an extremely lax regulator under military rule.

Military rule was gradually loosened between late 1977 and 1988. Between 1988 and 1991, Thailand enjoyed a brief period of democratic rule under the prime ministership of Chatichai Choonhavan. One of the consequences of democratization was that business interests from the provinces, which accounted for the vast majority of parliamentary seats, gained influence over policy making. These provincial businesspeople were primarily interested in channeling particularistic benefits to their supporters, with little regard for the implications for the consistency of policies important for economic growth.[18] They were also opposed to the insulation of technocrats, a preference that finally worked its way

[13] Bank of Thailand 1992, 298.
[14] Bank of Thailand 1992, 299.
[15] Bank of Thailand 1992, 300–301.
[16] Bank of Thailand 1992, 301.
[17] Bank of Thailand 1992, 301.
[18] Hicken 2001.

to the central bank. Whereas interfering in central bank appointments was generally considered off limits when the military was in control, Chatichai embarked on a significant departure from tradition. He fired the sitting central bank governor, Kamchorn Sathirakul. In 1990, he appointed an official who was known for his close ties to politicians, Vijit Supinit, to the governor's position.[19] Vijit's contribution to Thailand's weak regulatory performance is explored in the following sections of this chapter.

4.1.2 The Political Environment Following the Liberalization of Capital Flows

Most controls on capital flows in Thailand were dismantled in the course of 1992–93. The liberalization of capital flows in Thailand took place concomitantly with the final withdrawal of the military from political dominance. (The military had made a brief effort to return to power following Chatichai's term and withdrew with substantial loss of face following massive demonstrations.) Since 1992, as Chai-Anan Samudavanija puts it, "the armed forces have basically been trying to safeguard their military and security interests, including arms procurements. . . . [Officers] are convinced that their best strategy of survival is to keep away from direct political involvement and concentrate on the protection of the military's legitimate role and corporate interests. As long as parliamentary democracy continues to provide the formal rules of the political game and conventional coup making is therefore less feasible, military leaders and their cliques have to realign themselves with the leaders of political parties, and be seen as non-political, or at least non-partisan."[20]

Along with the withdrawal of the military, technocrats at the central bank increasingly became subject to the dictates of politicians. As far as the central bank is concerned, there was no legal obstacle to ensure insulation. Legally, the central bank governor reports to the finance minister, who can fire him at any time with cabinet approval.[21] As Chalongphob Sussangkarn, president of the Thailand Development Research Institute, sums up the common view of the post transition environment for financial decision-making, "elected politicians run everything."[22]

---

[19] *Asiamoney* February 1997, 17.
[20] Chai-anan 1997, 55.
[21] *Asiamoney* February 1997, 27.
[22] *Asiamoney* February 1997, 16.

Table 4.1 *Basic Electoral System Data*

	September 1992
Total districts	142
Three-seat districts	85
Two-seat districts	48
One-seat districts	9

Source: Hicken 1999, 7.

Who were these elected politicians who ran everything? In Thailand's bi-cameral parliamentary system, the upper house (the Senate) only had the power to delay legislation, and so the power to legislate rested almost entirely with the lower house (the House of Representatives). The leader of the party with the largest number of seats in the lower house assumed the office of prime minister. However, the electoral system ensured that the prime minister would have to rule in coalition with a number of other parties. The reasons were as follows.

Elections for the lower house were based on one-, two-, and three-member constituencies. Voters were allowed to vote for as many candidates as there were seats in their constituency, and the vote count was plurality based. There were no party lists.[23] As Table 4.1 shows, multiple-member constituencies accounted for the vast majority of seats in the September 1992 election.

Keeping in mind Duverger's Law and Cox (1997), we should expect a plurality-based electoral system that skews so sharply toward multiple member constituencies to generate a large number of parties.[24] This, in fact, was the case in the Thai context. Eleven parties were represented in parliament in the September 1992 election.

Under this system, Chuan Leekpai of the Democratic Party assumed office as the first post-transition prime minister in September 1992. In 1993, Chuan inaugurated the Bangkok International Banking Facilities, an offshore center for banks to borrow international funds, which opened the floodgates for capital inflows. Chuan remained in office until mid-1995, and was thus the chief executive who presided over the Thai economy during the critical early years following capital flow liberalization when international capital poured into the country.

[23] Anusorn 2000, 429.
[24] Cox 1997.

Chuan presided over a coalition with extremely diverse policy preferences. The Democratic Party was the only major party in Thailand whose core constituency had preferences over financial governance that were opposed to cronyism. This core consistency consisted of intellectuals and urban professionals in Bangkok and southern Thailand. This configuration has caused the party to be referred to as the "party of professors."[25] Any leader of the Democratic Party needed to be highly sensitive to the policy preferences of these core supporters to retain office. By and large, members of this core were upholders of the party's central "ideology" that it was "a party of deep rooted principles and integrity," and favored protecting financial technocrats from political interference.[26] There is little reason to believe that this group would have favored anything other than an extremely robust banking sector.

As a politician whose goal was to retain office, Chuan, however, did not have the luxury of sharing the preferences of the core group over banking sector robustness. The Democratic Party did not exclusively consist of the urban constituency described above; it also included a rural wing that was primarily concerned with particularistic benefits.[27] The views of this latter group could not be simply ignored by the party leadership, because the predominance of rural constituencies rendered it impossible for the Democrats to gain a significant number of parliamentary seats without a powerful rural base.[28] Senior members of this wing of the Democratic Party increasingly became engaged in illegal manipulations of the stock market in the 1990s.[29] The heaviest funders of illicit stock market transactions were weak finance companies, such as the politically connected Finance One group.[30] (Thanks to their heavy involvement in such transactions, the exposure of many finance companies to the stock market exceeded 60% of their equity funds.[31]) For this wing of the Democratic Party, the closure of undercapitalized finance companies would have meant substantial cutbacks in funding for speculative stock market transactions. The priorities of this latter wing thus placed its preferences over banking sector robustness far left of the center of the robustness continuum.

---

[25] King 1999, 211.
[26] McCargo 1997, 123.
[27] King 1999, 211–212.
[28] McCargo 1997, 123.
[29] Handley 1997, 108.
[30] Handley 1997, 101.
[31] Banyong and Supavud 1997, 10.

Given the above, any leader of the Democratic Party was under pressure to not diverge too far from the preferences of either of the two polarized groups. Consistent with these pressures, Chuan was widely perceived as a leader who, while personally honest, had policy preferences that represented a fine balance between the priorities of the two wings of his party.[32] (There is no evidence that Chuan had crony ties to bankers.) From this we can infer that Chuan, while not being an outright cronyistic official, was also no technocrat, and thus had preferences that were close to the middle of the robustness continuum.

The polarization of the support base that sustained Chuan in office was reinforced by the nature of Thailand's electoral system. The fragmentation of the vote generated by Thailand's electoral system meant that Chuan's Democratic Party was only able to assemble a majority by including many other parties in the cabinet.[33] The Democratic Party won 79 out of 360 seats in the house.[34] One of the coalition parties, the Palang Dharma Party, had an urban, educated constituency that was extremely sympathetic to the views of the technocratic wing of the Democratic Party. Palang Dharma controlled forty-seven seats,[35] which left a shortfall of fifty-four seats for a majority. This deficit could only be filled by forming a coalition with hard-line pork barrel parties like the New Aspiration Party, the Social Action Party, and the Chart Pattana Party. Leaders of the New Aspiration and Chart Pattana parties had strong links to stock market manipulators who relied heavily on weak finance companies for their funding.[36] In addition, Chart Pattana leaders were major shareholders in many weak finance companies.[37]

Based on the theory of this book, we should expect groups with cronyistic ties to the banking sector to have preferences over banking sector robustness that are sharply opposed to those who do not have such ties. (The former should be opposed to closing down weak financial institutions while the latter should be in favor of doing so.) Thus, Chuan's hold on prime ministerial office was critically contingent on making key appointments that did not displease groups with sharply polarized preferences on banking sector robustness, while his own preferences lay between the two.

[32] See Thailand interviews in the bibliography.
[33] Hicken 1999, 9.
[34] Anusorn 2000, 410.
[35] Anusorn 2000, 410.
[36] Handley 1997, 108.
[37] Lauridsen 1998, 148.

4.1.3 Chuan's Inner Circle of Banking Advisors

Whereas the finance ministry and the central bank operated fairly independently of each other under military rule, the finance ministry gained a far more prominent role in overseeing the central bank following democratization. Consistent with the need to satisfy his technocratically oriented supporters in parliament, Chuan appointed an official who represented their priorities to head the finance ministry. Correspondingly, consistent with the need to simultaneously please cronyistic members of his support base in parliament, Chuan reserved the central bank governorship for an official with strong crony associations.

Chuan appointed Tarrin Nimmanahaeminda to the post of finance minister. Tarrin had made his career at the Siam Commercial Bank, which was owned by the revered and scrupulously honest King of Thailand, and had risen to become the president and chief executive of this organization in 1984. When Chuan enticed Tarrin to relinquish this position to accept the position of finance minister, the news was welcomed by the Democratic Party's technocratically oriented core supporters.[38] Given his antecedents, and based on what I learned from interviews with several IMF officials who worked closely with him, I find little reason to believe that Tarrin's preference was for anything less than an extremely robust banking sector.[39]

At the opposite extreme with respect to crony links, Chuan chose to retain Vijit Supinit as the central bank governor. This choice was plainly aimed at pleasing the numerous parliamentarians who had close ties to weak banks. Vijit long had a reputation for being "close to politicians," especially those with ties to weak finance companies.[40] Asiamoney reports that there were "rumblings of dissatisfaction" about Vijit in the central bank, on the grounds that "his links with . . . [Chart Pattana party leader] Chatichai and other politicians created a conflict of interest."[41] (Recall that the Chart Pattana Party's leadership had close ties to weak finance companies.) Vijit was also considered to be extremely close to Banharn Silpa-Archa, a politician whose proclivity for pork barrel politics earned him the sobriquet of "the human cash machine." The relationship between Vijit and Banharn was so close that one press report referred to him as

---

[38] Pasuk and Baker 1997, 29.
[39] See interview list in the bibliography.
[40] *Asiamoney* February 1997, 17.
[41] *Asiamoney* May 1997, 16.

"Banharn's man."[42] Banharn's closest associates were deeply implicated not only in stock market manipulations, but also in pyramid schemes involving one of the weakest banks in Thailand's banking system, the Bangkok Bank of Commerce.[43] Vijit's close ties to politicians who relied on weak financial institutions for their speculative projects would indicate a preference for keeping these weak institutions open. This would amount to a preference for persisting with an extremely weak banking sector.

Another indication of Vijit's preferences comes from the fact that he engaged in battles of unprecedented intensity with proponents of stringent regulation, like Deputy Governor Ekamol Khiriawat.[44] Yet another indication comes from the resignation of another proponent of stringent regulation, the head of bank supervision Sirichai Sakornratanakul, on the grounds that he had been sidelined by the governor.[45]

In sum, thanks to the check to his power presented by a polarized parliament, Chuan had a finance minister and a central bank governor with highly polarized preferences over banking sector robustness while his own preferences lay between the two. This situation thus closely resembled the benchmark scenario for the signaling model with two signalers presented in Chapters 1 and 3. This scenario, it may be recalled, is associated with lax regulation despite the presence of a chief executive who does not have cronyistic links with bank owners. In the next section, I show that this, indeed, was the outcome.

4.1.4 The Bank Regulatory Environment Under Chuan

In March 1993, as mentioned earlier, the Chuan government inaugurated the Bangkok International Banking Facilities (BIBF), an offshore facility for commercial banks and finance companies to borrow from in foreign currencies.[46] With the opening of the BIBF, the foreign liabilities of banks as a proportion of the GDP jumped from 6 percent in 1992, to 11 percent in 1993, to 22 percent in 1994, and to a peak level of 28 percent in 1995.

A large proportion of these inflows was diverted to projects in the property sector. As Table 4.2 shows, finance companies played a leading role in the expansion of lending to the property sector between 1992 and 1995.[47]

---

[42] The quote is from Asiamoney February 1997, 17.
[43] Handley 1997, 108–109.
[44] *Asiamoney* February 1997, 13.
[45] *Asiamoney* February 1997, 16.
[46] Lauridsen 1998, 138.
[47] Bank of Thailand 1998b, 13.

Table 4.2 *Property Credits (Percent Change)*

	1992	1993	1994	1995
Real estate				
Finance companies	21.0	35.7	46.4	36.0
Commercial banks	21.2	21.0	19.9	9.9
TOTAL	21.1	25.8	29.2	20.2
Housing				
Finance companies	16.4	58.8	45.6	33.3
Commercial banks	32.3	36.5	35.4	21.1
TOTAL	30.6	38.7	36.6	22.6

Source: Bank of Thailand 1998b, 13.

Loans for housing extended by finance companies jumped by close to 60 percent in 1993 and by close to 50 percent in 1994. Commercial banks were not far behind, with housing loans increasing by over 30 percent per annum between 1992 and 1995.

While all of this information was publicly known, what was not publicly known was the precise degree to which banks were applying incoming funds to loans that had weak prospects for repayment in the early to mid-1990s. *Ex post*, it has become clear that a large proportion of loans, especially those by finance companies, fell into this category. It has also become clear that Chuan maintained a passive regulatory stance in the face of this increase in questionable loans.

Was Chuan's weak regulatory performance the consequence of gridlock generated by opposition to stringent regulation from cabinet partners? There are several reasons to believe that this was not the case. First, the problems in the banking sector during Chuan's term were still at a level that could be managed without seeking the approval of his cabinet, simply by implementing the powers already granted to the central bank by the various banking acts passed following the 1980s crisis. As for concerns about coalition collapse, it is hard to make the case that a minor tightening of enforcement of pre-existing rules would have seriously threatened Chuan's leadership of the coalition. Yet Chuan did not even undertake such a minor tightening. In addition, if it was truly gridlock rather than a lack of credible information that was stopping Chuan, we should at least observe some evidence that Chuan was aware of the problems in the banking sector. Consistent with an explanation based on information rather than gridlock, Chuan has consistently claimed that he was not aware. Why should we believe him?

Despite the powerful incentives for other political parties to come up with evidence challenging Chuan's claim, and the relative ease with which such information would be accessible to coalition partners like Chart Pattana, which later switched their allegiance, nobody has been successful in unearthing such evidence. Also consistent with a signaling explanation, there is evidence of deliberately misleading signals from Vijit, and disputes on this score with Tarrin, in the case of Thailand's **most** notorious bank collapse, that of the Bangkok Bank of Commerce (BBC). There is also evidence that Vijit had powerful personal incentives to suppress information about solvency problems in the finance company segment of the banking sector, and in fact this is what he did. I offer this evidence in the following paragraphs.

The BBC, Thailand's ninth largest bank, made massive loans to politicians to engage in a variety of pyramid schemes during Chuan's term. As Pasuk and Baker describe these schemes, politicians "took loans from the BBC to buy land, had the land revalued outrageously (times forty in some cases), then used it as collateral to take much larger loans from the BBC. They set up paper companies which borrowed from the BBC, then set up more companies which borrowed more loans to buy up the original companies and so on.... They took unsecured loans to buy up listed firms, then used further loan money to fan up their share prices in the hope of realizing a quick profit. They set up companies in offshore havens such as the Cayman Islands. These companies took loans from the BBC to buy up the group's existing holdings of shares at inflated prices."[48]

In response to a surge in loan defaults, the central bank ordered the BBC to increase its capital by Bt 800 million in 1992 and to undertake further increases in 1992–94.[49] These orders, however, fell far short of covering potential defaults. In 1993, a bank examination revealed that the BBC's nonperforming loans had risen to 40 percent, and the bank's de facto capital asset ratio was effectively negative.[50] The Bank of Thailand failed to take any action at this juncture, and by March 1994 the nonperforming loan problem had worsened with no commensurate increase in bank capital. In response to the 1994 data, the central bank ordered the BBC to increase bank capital by Bt 3 billion by June 1995.[51]

---

[48] Pasuk and Baker 1998, 107.
[49] *Nukul Report* 1998, 125.
[50] *Nukul Report* 1998, 125. Nonperforming loans, as per the prevailing definition, were loans on which no payments had been made for six months.
[51] *Nukul Report* 1998, 126.

Once again this was far from adequate to cover problem loans. The BBC finally collapsed in early 1996, a few months after Chuan left office.

In Pasuk and Baker's description of the regulatory failure over the BBC, the role of concealment of information (and therefore signaling) is extremely prominent. Recall Vijit's close ties to the Chart Thai party, whose senior members were heavily embroiled in the BBC's various pyramid schemes. As Pasuk and Baker describe Vijit's role in the regulatory failure, "he took personal charge of the [bank supervisors'] confidential reports and put them in his drawer."[52] In their place, as the *Bangkok Post* reports, he disseminated innocuous official reports that did not reveal the problems at the BBC.[53] Tarrin sent a memorandum to Vijit challenging the contents of his official reports.[54] The fact that this challenging memorandum was indeed received by Vijit was subsequently confirmed by the deputy governor of the central bank, Jaroong Nookhwun, and is reflected in central bank records.[55]

Recall that, in the model with two signalers with opposed preferences that differ from the chief executive's preference, a chief executive without close ties to the banking sector actually only registers a signal of a shock to defaults and responds to it if he gets an explicit signal from the second signaler confirming the shock. However, when the preferences of the signalers are sufficiently different, there is no confirmatory signal for any value of defaults, and the chief executive is vulnerable to failing to register default shocks altogether because he pays no attention to signals from his advisors. This, in turn, means that the advisors lose nothing from keeping the chief executive poorly informed, thereby completing the vicious circle. Consistent with what the model says we should expect under such conditions, Chuan has long claimed that he did not respond to the BBC's problems because he only became aware of the deterioration of the BBC after he had left office. There are two reasons why Chuan's claim is credible.

First, aside from the dispute over the veracity of reports described previously, even a committee appointed by the Chart Thai–led government, which was closely tied to the BBC, found "dishonest intention to evade the spirit of the law" on the part of the central bank when regulating

---

[52] Pasuk and Baker 1998, 108.
[53] "Vijit May Face Abuse Charge in BBC Case." *Bangkok Post* November 19, 1999.
[54] "Vijit May Face Abuse Charge in BBC Case." *Bangkok Post* November 19, 1999.
[55] "Vijit May Face Abuse Charge in BBC Case." *Bangkok Post* November 19, 1999.

the BBC.[56] The findings of this committee, chaired by former Finance Minister Suthee Singhasaneh, had long been suppressed by other parties, including the parties connected to Vijit; it was the Democrats who took the lead in publicizing the findings when they returned to office in the wake of the currency crisis.[57]

A second reason to believe Chuan is that, far from being defensive about the collapse of the BBC, it was Chuan who sought to make political capital of rumors about the BBC's true financial condition that began to emerge in May 1996. (By this time the Democratic Party had been in the opposition for several months.) In fact, the finance minister of the time, Surakiart Sathirathai of the Chart Thai Party, accused the Democratic Party of making matters worse for the BBC by making these rumors the subject of a censure debate in parliament.[58] Newspaper reports clearly reveal the Democratic Party to be on the offensive, and the parties closely tied to Vijit, the Chart Thai and Chart Pattana, also were on the defensive during this entire period.[59] Subsequently, when Chuan returned to power after the currency crash, he even approved efforts to initiate legal proceedings against Vijit for his role in the BBC fiasco.[60] If Chuan was complicit in the BBC fiasco, it would make far more sense for him to join with the other parties, which included numerous senior politicians with close financial ties to the BBC, to keep the true extent of the BBC's troubles secret or to at least not exacerbate its troubles by making them the subject of a censure debate.

There are good reasons to believe that Chuan, as claimed, was unaware of the true state of the finance company sector, too. Given the small sizes of finance companies, it is highly unlikely that Tarrin even got to see supervisory reports of these institutions. In effect, when it came to signaling the state of finance companies, Chuan had a single official signaler, Vijit. As the *Bangkok Post* reported on Vijit's role in suppressing information, "one central bank examiner said that Thailand's examination and supervision procedures, patterned after U.S. and British practices, were adequate for spotting weaknesses at local banks and finance companies.... [However] examiners were asked to 'tone down' the language used in official reports.'"[61]

[56] "Various Issues Obscure Reason Why Vijit Quit." *Bangkok Post* July 3, 1996.
[57] "Vijit May Face Abuse Charge in BBC Case." *Bangkok Post* November 19, 1997.
[58] "Finance Ministry Takes Over BBC." *Bangkok Post* May 18, 1996.
[59] "Finance Ministry Takes Over BBC." *Bangkok Post* May 18, 1996.
[60] "Vijit May Face Abuse Charge in BBC Case." *Bangkok Post* November 19, 1997.
[61] "Follow Up Action is What is Needed." *Bangkok Post* November 19, 1999.

Vijit appears to have had a strong vested interest in concealing the weak state of finance companies, as a means of avoiding their closure. As the *Bangkok Post* put it, "it was revealed that Vijit bought 40,000 shares in Siam City Credit Finance PLC at par. He was also accused of chairing a commission meeting to approve the listing of the company's shares. He later conceded selling the shares after the listing and making several million baht in profit."[62] (After Vijit's departure, Siam City Credit Finance was judged to be too weak to continue operating, and fraud proceedings were initiated against its senior managers.[63]) Given his unusually close ties with finance company owners, such as those of Siam City, aside from his ties with the Chart Pattana Party leadership, which had heavy stakes in this sector, Vijit would hardly be expected to give an accurate accounting of the weaknesses of the institutions in this sector to his chief executive. (After his resignation, Vijit became a senior advisor to the Chart Pattana Party.[64])

Finally, if any doubt remains about Vijit's ability to disseminate inaccurate information, it should be alleviated by a description of the episode involving the dismissal of Deputy Central Bank Governor Ekamol Khiriawat. Vijit had engineered Ekamol's dismissal by claiming that the latter, by all accounts a clean official who had disagreed with Vijit over several policy decisions, had leaked confidential information. In response to a defamation suit filed by Ekamol, Vijit was forced to apologize to Ekamol and beg for forgiveness for the false accusation in an advertisement in a mass circulation newspaper.[65]

Thus, a great deal of evidence supports Chuan's contention that he did not know, and that is why he did not seek to restore the robustness of the Thai banking sector in the years following capital flow liberalization. The theory of this book indicates why he did not know. Thanks to the political environment that he was operating in, which embodied checks on his power from parliament, Chuan did not have senior financial officials that he could entirely trust. Furthermore, given his lack of crony connections with bankers, he also did not have recourse to alternative ways of being well informed.[66]

---

[62] "Various Issues Obscure Reason Why Vijit Quit." *Bangkok Post* July 3, 1996.
[63] "Police Report Progress on Six Big Cases." *Bangkok Post* May 28, 1999.
[64] *Bangkok Post* November 19, 1997.
[65] "Apology to Ekamol Over Leak Allegation." *Bangkok Post* November 9, 1999.
[66] This latter way would, of course, have generated incentive problems.

4.1.5 Thailand After Chuan

Little was done to restore the robustness of the Thai banking sector in the 2 years between Chuan's departure and the onset of the Asian crisis. For the first of these years, the prime minister was Banharn Silpa-Archa of the Chart Thai Party, who led a short-lived coalition of pork barrel parties. There is little reason to believe that Banharn's preferences on banking sector robustness differed from his cronyistic preferences on other issues, especially given that his election campaign was heavily funded by one of the weakest financial institutions, none other than the Bangkok Bank of Commerce.[67] Banharn operated with two successive finance ministers, Surakiart and then Bodi Chunnananda, who were his close associates rather than distinguished technocrats. For most of his term his friend Vijit remained in the governor's post. In line with these arrangements, there is no evidence of signaling problems during Banharn's term. (Recall that it is not my claim that democracies will always have signaling problems.) In a cabinet where proponents of arm's length business government relations are not represented, there is little hope for efforts at increasing regulatory stringency, thanks to incentive problems. In fact, far from imposing stringent regulations, the Banharn administration attempted to bail out the BBC, pumping billions of baht into the organization prior to its final collapse.[68]

Banharn was succeeded as prime minister by former General Chavalit Yongchaiyudh. Information about the true state of the banking sector was no longer private by this time: Three hundred and fifty property companies had already filed for bankruptcy, exposing the extreme vulnerability of finance company loan portfolios.[69] So, signaling considerations are no longer pertinent for this period. Chavalit's coalition government consisted of six parties that had little inclination for technocratic governance. It was only when a currency crisis began to seem imminent that Chavalit finally attempted some reforms, involving the closure of a small number of finance companies. The coalition, however, included the Chart Pattana Party as the second largest party. As mentioned earlier, several senior members of this party had controlling interests in weak finance companies. They were thus unwilling to countenance any restructuring proposal that adversely affected their interests.[70] Instead, these

[67] Handley 1997, 109.
[68] *Bangkok Post* 11/19/99, "Vijit May Face Abuse Charge in BBC Case."
[69] Pasuk and Baker, 114.
[70] Haggard 2000, 53.

politicians were able to get the central bank governor to pump $11 billion into troubled finance companies via the Financial Institutions Development Fund.[71] In the words of the Nukul Commission, the Bank of Thailand "failed to insist on recapitalization as a means to rehabilitate their [i.e., the finance companies'] position. Also it did not tackle forthrightly the institutions' problem loans."[72] Furthermore, "having become a major creditor to these financial institutions, the fund failed to monitor them adequately."[73] This meant that these finance companies were left free to gamble for resurrection, by lending for even more speculative projects.

The massive injections of funds into finance companies also had wider repercussions for central bank governance. As Thai economists Yos Vajragupta and Pakorn Vichayanond put it, "these rescue attempts were in conflict with proper macroeconomic strategies, because given the narrow scope of the repurchase market where little sterilization can be conducted, those aid funds tended to enlarge money supply, fueling further spending and exacerbating both current account deficits and domestic inflation."[74]

Partly on account of these infusions, the Bank of Thailand was forced to preserve the exchange rate by running down its foreign reserves. These reserves were, however, small relative to Thailand's short-term debt, which had risen to exceed international reserves by this time.[75] The ongoing difficulties of the finance companies contributed to a sharp decline in the willingness of foreign lenders to roll over short-term debts. Speculative pressure on the baht also intensified by mid-1997, and this could have been an appropriate time to devalue. However, thanks to the weak bank regulatory performance of his predecessors as well as his own government, Chavalit was caught in a trap. The banking sector, especially the finance company segment, was much too undercapitalized to be able to withstand the jump in loan defaults that would follow from a devaluation. The banking sector was also much too undercapitalized to withstand the interest rate hikes that would follow from a currency defense. All that

---

[71] Nukul Commission Report 1998, 159–60.
[72] Nukul Commission 1998, 9.
[73] Nukul Commission Report 1998, 8.
[74] Vajragupta and Vichayanond 1998, 32. Vajragupta and Vichayanond empirically demonstrate that that the credits injected by the FIDF were strongly correlated to the expansion in the monetary base in the months leading up to the currency crisis.
[75] Corsetti et al. 1998.

was left by this point was to gamble on preserving the exchange rate by resorting to "accounting tricks."[76]

The trick was to secretly borrow billions of dollars via swap transactions and hide the fact that almost all the dollars held by the central bank were borrowed funds when reporting the reserve position. As Philippe Delhaise describes this maneuver, "it is an old trick used by rogue currency traders to conceal losses, but the volume involved in this case is beyond imagination, as a total of close to US$30 billion was involved.... Technically, that amount should have been deducted from official reserves which...had in reality fallen to about US$1.5 billion, close to technical insolvency."[77] Finally the baht was allowed to float on July 2, 1997, precipitating an exceedingly expensive rehabilitation of the banking sector, amounting to one-half of the country's GDP and several years of lost growth.[78]

To sum up, the checks on the chief executive's power over appointments presented by the legislature generated extreme signaling problems in the three years immediately following capital flow liberalization. The consequence was a severe deterioration in the bank regulatory environment, which was subsequently not reversed on account of incentive and gridlock problems. The outcome, of course, was Thailand's worst financial disaster that put its entire capital flow liberalization strategy in question.

4.2 SOUTH KOREA

Between capital flow liberalization in 1993 and the Asian currency crisis, South Korea's president was Kim Young Sam. In Section 4.2.1, I provide some background on the development model inherited by Kim from his military predecessors, displaying the ways in which this model rendered the banking sector vulnerable to collapse in the event of a shock to the interest rate. In Section 4.2.2, I describe the South Korean democratic political environment during Kim's term. In Section 4.2.3, I describe Kim's inner circle of banking advisors, and in Section 4.4.4, I assess the country's record of bank regulation in the wake of capital flow liberalization.

---

[76] Delhaise 1998, 89.
[77] Delhaise 1998, 89.
[78] Berg 1999.

4.2.1 Background

For over three decades prior to Kim Young Sam's election in 1992, the South Korean polity was controlled by the military. The country enjoyed remarkable economic success under military rule. Between 1965 and 1990, the per-capita gross national product (GNP) grew from less than $100 to over $5000.[79] This impressive growth record was achieved on the back of the remarkable export performance of massive conglomerates, known as *chaebol*. (The *chaebol* contributed up to three-quarters of the manufacturing GDP by the late 1980s.[80]) There were four critical aspects to the military's *chaebol*-based growth strategy that had a direct bearing on the robustness of the banking sector.

First, the government encouraged the *chaebol* to finance their investments with massive quantities of bank debt. It did so by directing state-controlled banks to lend large sums of money at low interest rates to conglomerates that were willing to conform to national priorities.[81] Even after the banks were privatized in the 1980s, the government continued to exercise substantial control over the deployment of loans. Over time, the share of debt to equity for Korean corporations rose to a ratio of approximately four to one, which was significantly higher than ratios seen anywhere else in the world.[82] As far as banks were concerned, the high debt carried by the *chaebol* rendered their ability to repay loans exceptionally sensitive to fluctuations in the interest rate.[83]

Second, the *chaebol* were allowed to enter into a wide variety of unrelated businesses. This need not have presented a problem if multiple market entries were based on careful profitability and cash flow considerations. However, when directing bank loans to finance such entries, the government focused almost exclusively on market share considerations. Consequently, Korea's corporations were among the least profitable in the region, generating a real return on assets of only 3.7 percent.[84] (The comparable number in Thailand was 9.8 percent, and in Indonesia 7.1 percent.) In effect, in Meredith Woo-Cummings' words, "the *chaebol* have courted a perpetual bankruptcy."[85] This meant that the banking sector,

---

[79] Moon and Lim 2001, 206.
[80] Noble and Ravenhill 2000 87.
[81] Woo-Cummings 1999, 120.
[82] Woo-Cummings 1999, 123.
[83] Wade and Veneroso 1998.
[84] Woo-Cummings 1999, 122.
[85] Woo-Cummings 1999, 122.

which had extended massive quantities of loans to the *chaebol*, was also courting a perpetual bankruptcy.

Third, under the Korean model, the *chaebol* were allowed to provide cross-guarantees from one firm within a group to another firm within the group when receiving loans. This meant that banks were inadequately diversified in terms of default risks.[86]

Fourth, until well into the 1990s, *chaebol* owners were not barred from conducting financial transactions under false names.[87] This meant that bankers were ill informed about the true levels of exposure of borrowers to financial risks, which rendered their loan portfolios all the more vulnerable to default.

I show that efforts to address these vulnerabilities following capital flow liberalization in 1993 fell well short of what was required to establish a stringent regulatory environment. I also show that major regulatory shortcomings can be attributed to the signaling environment.

4.2.2 The Political Environment Between 1992 and 1997

In the years following capital flow liberalization, South Korea had a freely elected president as well as a freely elected unicameral parliament. In South Korea's democracy, parliament has some notable powers. The president's deputy is called the prime minister, and his appointment must be approved by parliament. Parliament also has the power to recommend the removal of the prime minister, as well as any cabinet minister, by simple majority.[88] The parliament also has the power to impeach the president. These powers are aside from the usual powers commanded by most democratic parliaments, those of approving budgets and other legislation.

As far as the parties in parliament are concerned, in the words of Ahn Chung-si and Jaung Hoon, "nearly all Korean parties have one, and only one, social base, regionalism. This is the one social base, however, which is least likely to lead to a stable party system. The fact that regionalism predominates makes it naturally rather easy for regionally based politicians to build strong personalized support; this in turn prevents the parties from developing lively internal structures and from becoming as a result disciplined and stable. What emerges on the contrary is volatile bodies

---

[86] Delhaise 1998, 103.
[87] Oh 1999, 141.
[88] Yong-ho Kim 1998, 135.

plagued by factionalism."[89] On the one hand, the absence of party discipline and stability dilutes parliament's ability to serve as a major obstacle to the president's decision-making power. On the other hand, however, it places a burden on the president to take widely conflicting policy preferences of various parliamentary factions into account, because failure to do so could lead to the rapid departure of important parliamentarians from his party.

The constraints presented by factionalism were especially pronounced for Kim Young Sam, whose victory in the 1992 presidential election was the product of an opportunistic alliance between him and his military predecessor, Roh Tae Woo. In the 1980s, Kim was a well-known opponent of the military. However, in 1990, Kim accepted Roh's offer to merge his party into the ruling party in return for becoming the newly merged party's presidential candidate.[90] Given that his new party was an odd conglomeration of members of the previous regime and outsiders, Kim had to balance the interests of two polarized groups in parliament.

On the one hand, Kim had to retain the support of core members of his party, who had joined him in campaigning for democracy in prior decades. This called for distancing the new party from its military past. One aspect of this past was the close ties between the military regime and the *chaebol*. Thus, as a means of reinforcing his legitimacy in the eyes of his long-time supporters, Kim was under intense pressure to implement "measures to rein in the *chaebol*."[91] In concrete terms, reining in the *chaebol* meant eliminating false name transactions and cross-guarantees, cutting back on *chaebol* leverage ratios, and ensuring that loans would only be forthcoming for adequately profitable projects. These steps, in combination, were consonant with establishing an extremely robust banking sector.

Kim, however, did not have the luxury of focusing exclusively on legitimacy with democratic campaigners. He also had to retain the support of parliamentarians with ties to the previous regime who had close ties with the *chaebol*, as well as those who were concerned with the mundane business of winning elections. Whereas the motivations of the former are obvious, the attachment of the latter to the *chaebols* requires some explanation. Elections are extremely expensive affairs in Korea; the 1992 National Assembly and presidential election cost 5 trillion won

---

[89] Chung-Si and Hoon 1999, 151–52.
[90] Roh Tae Woo was constitutionally barred from running for re-election.
[91] Kang 2002, 198.

($5.1 billion), which amounted to 16 percent of the country's annual budget.[92] As David Kang has pointed out, "political funds in Korea came from business," which in Korea meant primarily the *chaebol*.[93] Kang has estimated that, between 1980 and 1987, the ten largest *chaebol* alone contributed at least 3.9 billion won to the ruling party.[94] These estimates do not include massive entertainment expenses that were undertaken on behalf of the ruling party by the *chaebol*. Given the importance of the *chaebol* for financial contributions, Kim was under intense pressure from members of his party to keep the *chaebol* well supplied with funds while making few changes in their mode of operation. This, of course, was consonant with having an extremely weak banking sector.

Assuming plausibly that Kim Young Sam's goal of remaining in office was best served by retaining control over his party, his preference would have been to balance these sharply opposed tendencies within his party. By implication, this would make him an official with only a moderate interest in reforming the *chaebols*, which amounts to a preference for a moderately robust banking sector.

4.2.3 Kim Young Sam's Inner Circle of Banking Advisors

When making key appointments, Kim Young Sam was under pressure to satisfy a parliament that was sharply polarized over the issue of reining in the *chaebol*. The checks to his power presented by parliament constrained Kim to give something to each extreme when making key financial appointments.

In Korea, the finance ministry was the conduit through which politicians directed banks to make loans to their favored *chaebol*. It was this role played by the finance ministry that has led it to be called "a powerful entity tainted with politics and longstanding relationships with the *chaebol*."[95] The finance ministry was also closely tied to the financial sector in another way. As Jin Wook Choi points out, "as of 1996, 357 former MOFE [ministry of finance and economy] bureaucrats took post retirement positions in the financial services industry. From 1997 to 1998, an additional 95 MOFE retired bureaucrats held top managerial positions in the financial sector."[96] In line with the preferences of the pro-*chaebol*

---

[92] Kang 2002, 194.
[93] Kang 2002, 196.
[94] Kang 2002, 196.
[95] Kirk 1999, 122.
[96] Choi 2002, 261.

Table 4.3 *Ministers of Finance and Economy Under Kim Young Sam*

Ministers of Finance and Economy	Tenure
Hong, Jae-hyung	12/94–12/95
Na, Wong-bae	12/95–8/96
Han, Seung-soo	8/96–3/97
Kang, Kyung-shik	3/97–11/97
Im, Chang-ryul	11/97–2/98

Source: Interviews by Abraham Kim.

elements in parliament, Kim Young Sam did nothing to challenge the ministry of finance's traditional orientation when making appointments. Instead of appointing a powerful reformer to break the ministry's close links to the *chaebol*, and giving him his support, Kim quickly and repeatedly turned over a series of finance ministers. The job was treated as a reward for political supporters, many with strong ties to the *chaebol*.[97] (Quick turnovers made it possible to reward as many supporters as possible.[98]) In the three years between December 1994 and December 1997, Kim had five ministers of finance. With such short terms in office, Kim's finance ministers had little opportunity, if they ever had the inclination, to alter the ministry's traditional pro-*chaebol* orientation (see Table 4.3).

In sharp contrast to his treatment of the leadership of the finance ministry, Kim Young Sam's treatment of central bank appointments was in line with the preferences of parliamentarians who favored *chaebol* reforms. He appointed respected technocrats to head the central bank and granted them his support for much longer terms in office than their counterparts in the finance ministry. Between March 1993 and August 1995, the central bank governor was Kim Myoung-ho. Since the mid-1980s, when he became the vice-superintendent of bank supervision, Kim Myoung-ho was at the forefront of efforts to rein in lending to the *chaebol*. While Kim Myoung-ho held this position, the Office of Bank Supervision attempted to force the *chaebol* to classify their businesses into two categories: mainstream and peripheral. One of the goals of the proposal was to then raise the robustness of banks by cutting off lending to peripheral, and thus

[97] For instance, Kang Kyong Shik, who took charge at a critical juncture in the crisis, was closely tied to the Samsung chaebol. See Chang 1998, 1557.
[98] Heo and Kim 2000, 502.

71

relatively weak, businesses.[99] Under Kim Myoung-ho, the Office of Bank Supervision also attempted to impose limits on cross-shareholdings and on real estate holdings, and also proposed that export-oriented projects, which were sacred cows in Korea's development model thanks to their contributions to economic growth, be subjected to credit controls.[100] Given that all these measures were aimed at significantly enhancing the robustness of banks, we can infer that Kim Myoung-ho's preference was for establishing an extremely robust banking sector.

Between August 1995 and December 1997, while the ministry of finance had five heads, the central bank had a single governor. This governor, Lee Kyong Shik, was noted for his immunity to the financial blandishments of the *chaebol*. John Oh describes Lee Kyong Shik as "an able economist who was reputed to be scrupulously honest and untainted by any hint of corruption."[101] Oh adds that "when Lee was a government official he brought home no more than his meager government salary, unlike many other officials who padded their incomes through illicit practices. Consequently, Lee's family lived in one of the many 'moon villages,' shanty towns that spread ever upward on mountainsides and where 'the moon rose first' but amenities were few and alleys were too steep and too narrow for vehicular traffic."[102] Lee's strictly arms' length relationship with the *chaebol* meant that he had no stake in perpetuating the system of feeding the *chaebol* with bank loans irrespective of the merits of their investment projects.

In sum, thanks to the checks on his power presented by parliament, Kim Young Sam's inner circle of banking advisors was sharply polarized in its preferences over banking sector robustness. Meanwhile, his own preferences lay between the two ends of the robustness continuum. This, as may be recalled, is the benchmark scenario for the signaling model in Chapter 3, which is associated with lax regulation. In the next section I show that the enforcement of bank regulations during Kim's term was consistent with the presence of such a signaling environment.

4.2.4 The Bank Regulatory Environment

The World Bank's ratings presented in Chapter 1 show that South Korea did not have a stringent bank regulatory environment. There are several

---

[99] Clifford 1998, 229.
[100] Clifford 1998, 229.
[101] Oh 1999, 133.
[102] Oh 1999, 133.

possible explanations for this failure. I argue in the following paragraphs that if one wishes to understand South Korea's regulatory record for the bulk of Kim Young Sam's term, the signaling explanation is the most plausible one.

First, MacIntyre and Haggard have argued that in the final months of Kim Young Sam's single term, when he was a lame duck, many parliamentarians gravitated to the party's presidential candidate, Lee Hoi Chang.[103] This made it exceptionally difficult for Kim to assemble majorities in the legislature, and the consequence was gridlock. Does a gridlock-based explanation for lax regulation seem plausible when applied to the bulk of Kim's term, which covers periods well before those covered in MacIntyre and Haggard's analysis? The record reveals that Kim was able to bypass obstacles to legislation for most of his term, even if it sometimes called for creative measures such as calling snap midnight sessions of parliament.[104] The severe shortcomings in bank regulation that were present well prior to late 1997 thus do not seem to be plausibly attributable to gridlock.

Another possible explanation is that Kim Young Sam was an unequivocal crony capitalist who all along favored *chaebol* interests, and thereby a weak banking sector. The fact that Kim's son was indicted for his illicit involvement in the collapse of a *chaebol*, Hanbo, would count as support for this view. The weakness of this view is that Kim undertook several modest regulatory measures that are uncharacteristic of an outright crony capitalist. Six months after assuming office, Kim Young Sam issued an emergency presidential order limiting financial transactions under false names.[105] Kim also initiated investigations into cross-shareholdings between *chaebol* companies and introduced some measures aimed at reining in lending to the *chaebol*.[106] Despite the limited impact of these reforms, John Oh points out that "the real name system [reforms], subsequently expanded to cover real estate transactions, has been seen as a lasting accomplishment of the Kim Young Sam government, despite subsequent ups and downs in implementation and partial de facto rescission."[107] Thus, the "Kim as unequivocal crony capitalist" argument is not entirely convincing either.

---

[103] Haggard and MacIntyre 2000.
[104] See Oh 1999.
[105] Oh 1999, 141.
[106] Smith 1998, 71.
[107] Oh 1999, 142.

In a third possible explanation, Donald Kirk writes that "Kim Young Sam, a bright government critic in the era of Park Chung Hee and Chun Doo Hwan, had displayed remarkable lack of understanding of economic issues since his election in December 1992."[108] This begs the question of why Kim, who by all accounts was an intelligent man, had a weak understanding of economic issues. One possible explanation is that he was uninterested in economics, which is hardly plausible given that he was the driving force in pressing for the globalization of Korea's economy and for the country's entry into the rich countries' club, the Organization for Economic Cooperation and Development (OECD).[109] The alternative and more compelling explanation for his lack of understanding is that he did not get useful advice from senior financial officials, which follows directly from the signaling perspective. I first summarize the specific nature of the regulatory failures under Kim, and then show why they are consistent with a signaling-based perspective.

During Kim Young Sam's term, there was a massive binge of over-borrowing and overinvesting on the part of the *chaebol*. In 1993, the four largest *chaebol* incurred debts of 12.4 trillion won. These debts reached 25.5 trillion won by mid-1997. Between 1991 and mid-1997, borrowing by the top thirty *chaebol* increased by over 30 percent, raising the debt–equity ratio from 400 to 450 percent.[110] As far as the prospects for repayment to banks were concerned, the top thirty *chaebols'* profits by the end of 1996 amounted to only 2.8 percent.[111] (Low profits are indicative of a high propensity for loan defaults.)

While disagreements continue over many contending explanations for the borrowing binge of the 1990s, there is a remarkable degree of agreement on one cause: The country's merchant banks, which are financial institutions that are not allowed to take direct deposits, played a leading role in this binge and contributed substantially to the crisis. There were thirty such institutions in the years following capital flow liberalization. In addition to the six merchant banks that existed prior to capital flow liberalization, nine were given licenses in 1994, and fifteen in 1996.[112] Unlike with commercial banks, there were few restrictions on *chaebol* ownership

---

[108] Kirk 1999, 23.
[109] Oh 1999, 150–51.
[110] Noble and Ravenhill 2000, 85. Moon and Kim 2000, 152.
[111] Moon and Kim 2000, 152.
[112] Noble and Ravenhill 2000, 94.

of merchant banks. Supervisory responsibility for these institutions was shared between the Ministry of Finance and Economy (MOFE) and the Office of Bank Supervision (OBS) at the central bank, with the former being the dominant partner.[113]

As Hahm and Mishkin point out, the supervision of the merchant banks was exceedingly lax. In their words, "without tight supervisory regulation the merchant banking corporations engaged in increasingly risky business and exposed themselves to significant interest rate, currency and credit risks. . . . The loan concentration to big business conglomerates (*chaebol*) was relatively high; they often borrowed short-term at low interest rates and invested in relatively long-term high yield assets; and they even engaged in various off-balance sheet transactions related with risky offshore, lower credit country products."[114] The short-term foreign debts of the merchant banks, amounting to $12 billion by 1997, accounted for two-thirds of their foreign debt.[115] In the case of one-half of them, short-term financing accounted for 93 percent of their total financing.[116] In contrast, over 80 percent of their lending was long-term. Given the heavy concentration of their lending to *chaebol* that were earning low profits, this meant that the merchant banks were not only highly vulnerable to insolvency thanks to potential defaults, but also to illiquidity in the event that short-term loans were not rolled over.

The binge in short-term borrowing by the merchant banks helped push the share of short-term foreign debts in South Korea from 44 percent in 1993 to 58 percent of the total foreign debts in 1996.[117] The most significant consequence of this skew toward short-term borrowing was that South Korea ended up accumulating short-term debt that amounted to double the value of foreign reserves by 1997, thus leaving the country vulnerable to a sharp forced devaluation.[118] Given that the country had increased its foreign debt from $44 billion to $120 billion between 1993 and 1997, the prospect of a devaluation implied a high level of expected defaults. Thus, the liquidity position of the merchant banks was closely related to the solvency of the banking sector as a whole.

---

[113] Noble and Ravenhill 2000, 94.
[114] Hahm and Mishkin 1999, 16–17.
[115] Choi 2002, 261.
[116] Choi 2002, 261.
[117] Ha-Joon Chang 1998, 1556.
[118] Corsetti et al. 1998.

Despite the importance of bolstering the capitalization of commercial banks under such conditions, this area of regulation was also characterized by inertia. The central bank's Office of Bank Supervision, while nominally responsible for supervising commercial banks, was de facto subordinate to the finance ministry in this area, too.[119] The OBS got minimal support from the MOFE to stringently enforce capital asset regulations on commercial banks. The central bank had introduced rules calling for all banks to meet the international capital asset ratio standard of 8 percent.[120] However, 46 percent of the country's twenty-six commercial banks did not comply.[121] The banks that did not comply included two of the country's largest banks, Korea First Bank and Seoul Bank.[122]

Is it possible that the MOFE and the central bank were unaware of the sharp deterioration in the position of merchant banks and the associated risks to the solvency of the entire banking sector? This was patently not the case. As Jin Wook Choi has pointed out, the central bank brought the fragility of the merchant banks to the attention of the finance ministry eighteen times between 1995 and 1997.[123]

Recall that, when there are two signalers with opposed preferences that are far from the chief executive's preference, the chief executive has a propensity for failing to register or to at least underestimate a default shock. Just as in the Thai case, we should expect to see differences in signals about the state of vulnerability of banks among the signalers and evidence that the chief executive did not know the true state of vulnerability. Also as in the Thai case, there is much evidence of this nature, with the finance minister in this case taking the role (analogous to Vijit in Thailand) of suppressing information and the central bank challenging this strategy.

By late 1996, some of the weakest *chaebol* had already begun to declare their inability to repay loans, thereby damaging the ability of merchant banks and commercial banks to repay their foreign creditors. This, in turn, raised the likelihood that short-term lenders would refuse to roll over their loans. As the central bank tried hard to communicate, it is apparent that there was a sharp jump in expected defaults in early 1997. Despite this extreme danger, accounts of this period display a president

---

[119] Choi 2002, 264.
[120] Smith 1998, 74.
[121] Smith 1998, 74.
[122] Smith 1998, 74.
[123] Choi 2002, 264.

who was exclusively focused on the legal problems of his son, who was being investigated for corrupt transactions involving the *chaebol*, Hanbo, at this time.[124]

While it is understandable that the president would be distracted by this scandal, it is clear that senior financial advisors were also responsible for the president's failure to focus on financial matters. Under pressure from the central bank to alert the president, the Finance Minster "Kang [Kyong Shik] reportedly said that the president should not be further troubled 'while the country was already disturbed with the Hanbo scandal'."[125] When the central bank sent a direct signal to the president alerting him of an impeding foreign exchange crisis, which would of course have disastrous implications for bank balance sheets, the finance minister refused to confirm the signal, instead downplaying the dangers.[126] As John Oh points out, "simply astounding was the news that Finance-Economy Minister Kang Kyong Shik and presidential Economy Secretary Kim In Ho had suppressed and buried reports their subordinates had submitted warning of an approaching foreign loan crisis."[127]

Following the onset of the currency crisis, Kang Kyong Shik and Kim In Ho were imprisoned for "dereliction of duty and malfeasance."[128] While some have claimed that this was a case of unfair scapegoating, two points are worthy of note. First, the reasons given were explicitly informational; in the words of the government's deputy spokesman, "Kang failed to warn the government in time and should take responsibility for worsening the situation."[129] Second, since the prosecution was pursued by Kim Young Sam's successor, Kim Dae Jung, rather than by Kim Young Sam himself, there is no obvious reason why the latter should not also have been jailed if he knew the true picture and still did not act. This would hardly have been unusual in the Korean context, given that Kim Young Sam had been extremely aggressive in prosecuting his predecessors as chief executive and had gained popularity from doing so.

A final reason to believe that problems in credible communication were part of the problem comes from the fact that it actually finally took a

---

[124] Following an investigation that continued through the first half of 1997, Kim Young Sam's son, Kim Hyun Chul, was finally sentenced to three years in prison in October 1997. See Heo and Kim 2000, 503.

[125] Oh 1999, 223.

[126] Moon and Lim 2001, 222.

[127] Oh 1999, 223.

[128] *Far Eastern Economic Review* September 10, 1998, 21.

[129] *Far Eastern Economic Review* September 10, 1998, 21.

phone call in late November 1997 from President Bill Clinton, with whom Kim Young Sam had a rapport, to persuade Kim that his country was indeed on the verge of a financial meltdown.[130] (Clinton had been alerted by the IMF.) The fact that it took the president of another country to persuade Kim suggests the depth of the problems in credible signaling generated by the Korean domestic political environment. Thus, signaling considerations appear to have played a prominent role from fairly early to fairly late in the trajectory of Korea's downfall.

This is not to say that gridlock did not also play a role late in Kim's term. (Recall that Chapter 3 shows how gridlock can exacerbate the effects of incredible signaling.) Haggard and MacIntyre have well described how conflicts between the factions of Kim Young Sam and Lee Hoi Chang contributed to the failure to pass legislation that would have tightened the bank regulatory environment in November 1997.[131] A group of advisors had proposed that all financial supervision be placed under the control of a newly created, independent Financial Supervision Board. Because the ruling party had a majority in the legislature, Kim and Lee could have pushed through the necessary legislation if they had come to agreement over the urgent need for reform and commanded a united party. On the one hand, as described previously, Kim displayed little awareness of the need for urgent reforms. (Lee, from his position outside the government, appears to have been as poorly informed.) To make matters even worse, the proposed legislation necessarily called for dismissing some employees of the Bank of Korea and the Ministry for Finance and Economy, and thus potentially losing electoral support among union members. This made it difficult for Lee to agree to the proposed legislation, especially since his main opponent, Kim Dae Jung, had a strong support base among union members. The legislation was thus shelved on November 16.[132]

The decision to postpone essential financial reform legislation was very poorly received by international financial markets. From the day that the financial legislation was postponed, for three days straight, the won plunged to the bottom of its trading band. On the third day, this plunge took ten minutes, prompting a premature end to foreign currency trading. Finally, the central bank abandoned its defense of

---

[130] Moon and Kim 2001, 222.
[131] Haggard and MacIntyre 2000.
[132] Haggard 2000, 58.

the won on November 21, an event that was treated as a national disgrace.[133]

A month later, in the wake of mass layoffs precipitated by the devaluation, Kim Dae Jung defeated Lee Hoi Chang to grasp the presidency. The opposition parties granted Kim Dae Jung immense powers to help Korea recover from the crisis. He also did not have cronyistic ties to the *chaebol*. In sum, Korea now had a president with a preference for a robust banking sector temporarily operating in an environment where parliament did not serve as a check on his power. As the theory predicts, and as Haggard has showed in detail, this was a period of major improvements in bank regulation in South Korea. Between December 22 and 30 alone, thirteen acts relating to the financial sector were passed, including one creating a new financial regulatory agency that was granted substantial powers.[134]

To sum up, consistent with the argument of this book, democratic South Korea was vulnerable to signaling problems, and these problems were associated with the presence of a lax regulatory environment.

4.3 THE PHILIPPINES

This case study is in three sections. Section 4.3.1, a background section, addresses the two decades prior to capital flow liberalization in 1992. I divide these years into two periods, an authoritarian period and a democratic period. In the first of these periods, between 1972 and 1986, the Philippines was under the control of the notoriously cronyistic dictator, Ferdinand Marcos. In the second of these periods, between 1986 and 1992, the Philippines was a democracy with Corazon Aquino as president. I then move, in Section 4.3.2, to describing the political environment in the Philippines after capital flows were liberalized, when Fidel Ramos was president. Section 4.3.3 addresses bank regulation under Marcos.

4.3.1 Background: The Philippines Prior to Capital Flow Liberalization

4.3.1.1 Bank Regulation Between 1972 and 1986. From 1972 to 1986, the Philippines was under the authoritarian rule of Ferdinand Marcos. Marcos' close ties to the banking sector have been exhaustively

---

[133] Haggard 2000, 58.
[134] Haggard 2000, 101–2.

documented in many contributions to the literature and will not be repeated here.[135] In the Philippines, bank supervision is predominantly controlled by the central bank.[136] Marcos was unconstrained in appointing officials who shared his cronyistic preferences to head the central bank. Furthermore, being a dictator, Marcos was also unimpeded by legislative gridlock from implementing his policy preferences. I show in the following paragraphs that the outcome, as the theory indicates, was in accord with Marcos' cronyistic preferences, namely, a lax bank regulatory environment.

During most of Marcos' authoritarian tenure, the central bank governor was Gregorio Licaros. As Kunio Yoshihara describes it, Marcos' appointment of Licaros to this position was due to his "apparently liking his subservient attitude."[137] He goes on to add that, "during his twelve year tenure at the bank, it is said that he [Licaros] made the bank's facilities available for not only Marcos, but also for a number of his own clients in the private sector. Many allegations of corruption have been hurled against him; he is said to be the most corrupt governor in the bank's history."[138]

In such an environment we should expect to see no evidence of signaling problems, and we should expect bank regulation to be exceedingly lax, in line with the chief executive's preferences. This, in fact, was the case. As Philippine economist Maria Socorro Gochoco-Bautista puts it, "rules on the treatment of past due loans, the provisioning of reserves versus bad loans, and the examination of deposits by central bank examiners continued to be either or both weak and inadequately enforced."[139] The enforcement of rules on lending to directors, officers, stockholders and related interests was also exceedingly lax. On top of all this, the capital asset ratio minimum was actually cut by almost two-thirds, from 15 to 6 percent, and was also poorly enforced.[140]

The most egregious acts of weak regulation occurred with respect to two large state-owned banks, the Philippine National Bank (PNB) and the

---

[135] For an excellent book on this subject see Paul Hutchcroft's *Booty Capitalism* 1998a.

[136] This situation was later mildly altered with the granting of limited supervision powers to the Philippine Deposit Insurance Corporation in the early 1990s. As will become apparent, this has no bearing on our argument.

[137] Yoshihara 1994, 73.

[138] Yoshihara 1994, 73.

[139] Gochoco-Bautista 2000, 36.

[140] Gochoco-Bautista 2000, 39.

Development Bank of the Philippines (DBP). These banks were allowed to divert vast loans, without regard to the prospects for repayment, to Marcos' close cronies.[141] This was a category of loans that became so large that they spawned a technical term, behest loans. At one point, it was estimated that forty-four out of eighty-seven nonperforming loans of more than $5 million were made at the direct request of Marcos.[142]

The consequence of massive behest lending was that both the Philippine National Bank and the Development Bank of the Philippines became technically insolvent. It was revealed that 90 percent of the loan portfolio of the Development Bank of the Philippines and 50 percent of the portfolio of the Philippine National Bank were nonperforming. In the case of the Philippine National Bank, which was the nation's largest bank, the scale of the problem was so huge that rehabilitation ended up costing approximately 10 percent of the country's GDP.[143]

It should be noted that the central bank also performed banking functions during Marcos' rule. The central bank was encouraged to liberally loan funds to rural banks via its rediscount window, without subjecting these loans to appropriate risk analysis. Many of these loans went into default, resulting in massive losses for the central bank.[144] In addition to the above, the central bank was forced to assume the foreign exchange risk, and absorb the foreign exchange liabilities, of several politically connected business people. These commitments generated massive losses when the peso slumped in the 1980s.[145]

In 1981, the flight of a businessman with an unsecured debt worth $100 million triggered a crisis of confidence in the banking sector. Several investors withdrew their money from financial institutions. Worst affected were the finance companies, which had lent the largest proportions of their loans to high-risk borrowers. As a consequence of bank runs, several major finance companies went bankrupt. In light of Licaros' weak response to the financial crisis, the IMF pressured Marcos for a change of leadership at the central bank.[146] In response, Marcos replaced Licaros with Jaime Laya, who was well known for having a close relationship with Marcos.[147]

---

[141] Intal and Llanto 1998, 8–9.
[142] Haggard 1990, 234.
[143] Delhaise 1998, 167.
[144] Intal and Llanto 1998, 9.
[145] Intal and Llanto 1998, 12.
[146] Broad 1988, 90.
[147] Interview with Ernest Leung June 3, 1999.

After three years with few significant improvements in prudential regulation, combined with massive bailouts of Marcos cronies, Laya made a major policy error.[148] In 1984, the Philippine economy was in the doldrums with a 7 percent contraction in a single year. The currency was under severe downward pressure, and the central bank was rapidly running out of foreign reserves. In response to this crisis, Governor Laya followed Marcos' instructions to report false foreign reserve statistics. In response, the international financial institutions forced Marcos to fire Laya.

Laya's replacement was Jose "Jobo" Fernandez. While Fernandez was not considered to be as close to Marcos as Laya, he can hardly be considered to be an official who had arm's length ties to the banking sector. Fernandez was the head of one of the Philippines' largest commercial banks, the Far East Bank and Trust Company. It is widely believed that he did not relinquish his financial ties to this institution even after he assumed the governorship.[149] Fernandez was also exceptionally well acquainted with the owners of other large private banks in the system by virtue of the fact that he had served as the president of the Bankers' Association of the Philippines, which is dominated by major privately owned financial institutions. Consistent with these connections, Fernandez did not move to tighten the prudential regulation of the largest banks in the system, failing to even impose a minimum capital asset ratio standard. Instead, Fernandez focused his early efforts on the closure of small and moderately sized institutions in the system, often choosing which institutions to close and to spare on the basis of arbitrary criteria.[150] Between 1984 and 1986, Fernandez closed down twenty-two thrifts and seventy-two rural banks.[151] He also closed down two medium-sized commercial banks. Aside from the closure of one financial institution that had ties to Marcos, it is hard to make the case that Fernandez's actions were not in accord with Marcos' preferences. It was with this record that Fernandez moved into the second part of his term as central bank governor under a new president, Corazon Aquino.

---

[148] Hutchcroft 1998a, 152–55 describes Laya's bail outs in detail.

[149] Hutchcroft 1998a describes how the profits of the Far East Bank and Trust Company grew enormously during his governorship, provoking accusations of conflict of interest.

[150] Hutchcroft 1998a details the accusations made against Fernandez about his nontransparent criteria for closing financial institutions.

[151] Philippine Deposit Insurance Corporation, 1999 (www.pdic.gov.ph).

4.3.1.2 Bank Regulation Between 1986 and 1992. In 1986, follow-ing a mass public uprising in the wake of rigged elections, Marcos was forced to leave office. (Since the events leading up to this uprising have been well documented elsewhere, and are not directly pertinent to the argument of this book, I do not describe them here.[152]) Corazon Aquino, the leader of the opposition, assumed the presidency. In the fol-lowing year, the Philippines adopted a new constitution, which estab-lished a presidential and unitary form of democracy. Presidents were to be elected every six years from a national constituency. The new con-stitution also established a bicameral congress, based on first past the post-elections.

The new president, Aquino, was far from being a Marcos-style crony capitalist. There is thus little reason to believe that she would have a preference for compromising the robustness of the banking sector in the interest of large banks. However, she was forced to operate with a central bank governor with close ties to large banks.

Recall that bank regulation in the Philippines fell under the control of the central bank governor. (Because he did not report to the finance minister, the latter did not have a line responsibility for bank regulation.) Retaining Fernandez as central bank governor thus effectively meant that he would be the one with the responsibility of signaling Aquino on the state of the banking sector. Senior members of a business coalition known as the Makati Business Club insisted on the retention of Fernandez until the end of his term at the end of the decade.[153] (Recall that Fernandez was a major figure in the business community prior to assuming his position.) This club of wealthy businessmen had played a central role in financing widespread demonstrations that placed Aquino in office and was also immensely influential in Congress. Aquino, whose ability to get an alter-native candidate approved by the legislature over the objections of the Makati group was highly questionable, ended up retaining Fernandez as governor.

In sum, the Philippines under Aquino had a chief executive who was not financially connected to large banks, and thus had no incentive to compromise bank regulation and banking sector robustness to benefit them, and a central bank governor who did have such incentives. The theory of this book indicates that when a chief executive is forced to

---

[152] See, for example, Thompson 1995.
[153] Hutchcroft 1998a, 185.

rely on a signaler with preferences on banking sector robustness that are significantly different from her own, she is likely to receive incredible signals and is consequently vulnerable to failure in creating a stringent regulatory environment. This meant that even though Aquino was not a crony capitalist leader, the democratic Philippines was still vulnerable to having a bank regulatory environment that was not stringent.

Confirmation of the signaling perspective comes from the fact that, even when Fernandez, signaling a banking sector in dire straits, recommended a dramatic tightening of prudential reforms, Aquino virtually ignored his signal in its entirety. (Recall from Chapter 3 that when the preferences of the central bank governor and the chief executive are sufficiently different, the latter will assume that all signals are simply part of the governor's randomization strategy and not respond.) Aquino was not impeded by legislative gridlock in the regulatory realm early in her term, because she had access to a number of decree powers prior to the seating of a democratically elected legislature. Thus, if she wished, Aquino could easily have approved the nineteen changes to the banking laws recommended by Fernandez in June 1987, a few weeks prior to the seating of the legislature. As it turns out, she refused to act on seventeen of them, in effect disbelieving Fernandez's signal that the banking sector was so weak as to justify immediate major reforms.[154]

Consistent with the signaling model, the regional literature suggests that Fernandez's low credibility in the eyes of Aquino and key advisors meant that his proposals were received with great skepticism; as Paul Hutchcroft points out, "distrust of the central bank – and of Fernandez in particular – is a plausible explanation for why Aquino failed to use her decree powers to implement major prudential reforms."[155]

Whereas signaling issues served as the primary obstacle to reform early in Aquino's term, once the new legislature was elected, it is apparent that legislative gridlock also hampered essential reforms. As Heller, Keefer, and McCubbins put it, "the 1987 constitution instituted an American style presidential system with substantial new controls on executive power. Aquino's failure to build a legislative coalition in Congress exacerbated the gridlock created by multiple veto gates and placed severe limitations on her own authority. Divided government was a key factor undermining the effectiveness of her government. At the end of her time in the

---

[154] Hutchcroft 1998a, 193.
[155] Hutchcroft 1998a, 193 fn 45.

presidency, Corazon Aquino had made only modest progress in economic reform."[156]

In light of these arguments, improvements in the robustness of the banking sector in the Aquino presidency took a highly circumscribed form. They consisted almost entirely of profit handouts to large banks, which is hardly a long-term solution to banking sector weakness, and the closure of weak small banks. Major prudential reforms involving the entire banking sector are notable in their absence.

As far as the handouts to large banks are concerned, Paul Hutchcroft has provided the most concise description of this aspect of Fernandez's record. In his words: "In the late 1980s and early 1990s high interest, low risk treasury bills became the major pot of gold, as commercial banks came to be major lenders to the government; by 1990 the value of outstanding government securities actually exceeded the value of all bank deposits. A few chosen banks were given lucrative monopoly privileges over the sale of these securities. An additional source of riches was available in the 1980s to an even smaller number of banks lucky enough to be chosen as the depositories of government funds. Using these low or no cost funds the banks could turn around and invest in government securities yielding 20 percent interest and more. In other words funds borrowed from the government were re-lent to the government at much higher rates. Drawing on these rich lodes of privilege, the five largest private domestic commercial banks increased their share of total system-wide assets from 22.1 percent in 1980 to 26.4 percent in 1985 and 38 percent in 1990. Their position was assisted not only by government handouts, but also by the failure of the central bank to stand in the way of collusive practices among the banks. . . . Because of the handsome advantages that they enjoyed, the banks prospered as the economy faltered. Between 1990 and 1993, the commercial banks averaged 17.9 percent annual growth in total assets and nearly 20 percent return on equity – while GDP grew at the rate of only 1 percent."[157]

As mentioned previously, alongside providing handouts to large banks, Fernandez continued on his program of closing down small financial institutions. Between 1987 and 1990, he closed down seven thrifts and forty-four rural banks.[158] There are some indications that Fernandez was not immune to ensuring that he benefited from these reforms. He was accused

---

[156] Heller, Drake, and McCubbins 1998, 167.
[157] Hutchcroft 1999, 169.
[158] PDIC 1999.

of rigging bids for closed down financial institutions, in favor of a large bank in which he personally held a substantial share.[159] The gains made by Fernandez's bank eventually provoked an internal inquiry within the central bank. While the results are confidential, I received strong indications, in interviews with senior central bank officials, that the inquiry did not entirely clear Fernandez.[160]

In sum, even with the transition to a chief executive with a preference for reform, the Philippine regulatory environment did not become stringent. This failure is plausibly explained initially exclusively by the absence of credibility of Fernandez as a signaler, and subsequently also by gridlock.

4.3.2 The Political Environment in the Philippines After Capital Flow Liberalization

The Philippines had its first democratic election since Marcos' departure in 1992. The winner was former general Fidel Ramos. An exceptional set of circumstances following Ramos' ascension meant that the president was able to carve out a realm of policy making that was immune to legislative checks. In brief, with the help of the international financial institutions, Ramos undertook what may be fairly termed an "executive grab" of the central bank.

The central bank, thanks to the losses incurred by Marcos' governance decisions, had been severely hampered in performing basic open market operations in the course of the late 1980s and early 1990s. Consequently, international organizations as well as domestic technocrats saw it as essential to close down the old central bank and replace it with a new monetary authority. Thus, the new democratic constitution, which was adopted in 1987 in the wake of Marcos' departure, set out as a goal that "Congress shall establish an independent central bank...[that] shall provide policy direction in the areas of money, banking, and credit."[161]

The Philippine legislature was, however, reluctant to implement this provision without gaining significant powers of oversight.[162] Most importantly, legislators wanted to use this provision to gain the right to screen the budgets of the central bank. Central bankers were reluctant

---

[159] Hutchcroft 1998a, 181.
[160] Anonymous interviews, June 2, 1998.
[161] Philippine Constitution (1987) Section 20, Article XII.
[162] Hutchcroft 1998a, 198.

to accept "independence" on these terms. With his ascent to the presidency in 1992, Ramos embarked on massive efforts to break this deadlock. In this he was helped by the World Bank, which made the closure of the old central bank a condition for disbursing a badly needed financial sector adjustment loan of $450 million.[163] After distributing massive amounts of pork to legislators, Ramos was finally successful in pushing the New Central Bank Act through the legislature in June 1993.[164] This Act ordered the closure of the Central Bank of the Philippines and approved its replacement by a new central bank called the Bangko Sentral ng Pilipinas. While the Act did call the new central bank independent, a close examination of legal provisions reveals that the grant of "independence" actually amounted to granting the chief executive control over the institution.

As a by-product of the establishment of a new "independent' central bank, the president secured the power to appoint a governor of his choice. He was also allowed to replace the governor without congressional approval on the vaguest of criteria. (These criteria included shortcomings with respect to "moral character," "integrity," "probity and patriotism," and "competence in social and economic disciplines."[165]) The New Central Bank Act did not grant the legislature the right to screen central bank budgets. In sum, the Act gave the legislature virtually no powers of oversight over the central bank. In effect, Ramos had succeeded in using a highly unusual set of circumstances involving the replacement of a central bank, which seldom occurs, to carve out a significant realm of policy where he faced few checks on his power.

In this new institutional environment, Ramos was unconstrained in appointing a childhood friend, Gabriel Singson, to the governorship. My extensive interviews in the Philippines reveal a widespread perception that Singson was far from being the best-qualified candidate for the job but was appointed primarily because he was trusted by the president.[166]

In effect, the closure of a central bank, and its replacement by a brand new entity that was protected to a significant degree from legislative scrutiny, allowed Ramos to avoid signaling problems in a democratic

---

[163] Hutchcroft 1998a, 208.

[164] Hutchcroft 1998a, 208.

[165] New Central Bank Act, 3–4.

[166] Many people on my interview list, including those who familiarly referred to Singson as "Gaby," made this claim. However, since Singson was still governor during my field trip, all statements were not for attribution.

context.[167] (Recall that it is not my claim that democracies will always have signaling problems.) However, despite the absence of signaling problems, Ramos was unable to establish a stringent regulatory environment. As I show in the next section, this was because legislative gridlock obstructed the passage of critical reforms in regulatory realms not covered by the New Central Bank Act.

4.3.3 Bank Regulation in the Wake of Capital Flow Liberalization

The power to enforce a high capital asset ratio fell well within the realm of the central bank as per the New Central Bank Act. In 1992, concomitant with capital flow liberalization, the central bank had begun to demand capital asset ratio statistics for the first time in nearly a decade. In September 1993, after the new central bank was established, the reporting of capital asset ratios was raised to the status of a quarterly requirement.[168] A capital asset ratio of 17 percent was enforced, which was adequate to cover expected defaults.[169] As for the consequences, in Ponciliano Intal's words, "the relatively high capital asset ratio of Philippine banks is one reason why the Philippine banking sector has been able to weather the East Asian crisis relatively comfortably."[170]

What role did bank regulation play in this? Some have argued that relatively low capital inflows, combined with the profit handouts given to banks prior to capital flow liberalization, largely account for the robustness of the Philippine banking sector following liberalization.[171] To some extent, such arguments are valid. Capital inflows into Philippine banks indeed gained momentum somewhat later than for other countries in the region, only jumping from 9 percent of the GDP to 17 percent of the GDP in 1996. (By way of comparison, Thailand's inflows amounted to over 20 percent of the GDP from 1994 onward.) It is also the case that, thanks to high profits generated by Fernandez's policies, the Philippine banking sector embarked on capital flow liberalization with a high capital–asset

---

[167] Note that the Philippine Deposit Insurance Corporation, which was placed under the control of the finance minister, also had some limited supervisory responsibilities. However, this is irrelevant for our purposes, since it is sufficient for a chief executive to have one signaler who shares his preferences for there to be no signaling problem.

[168] Bangko Sentral ng Pilipinas 1999, 40.

[169] For the capital asset ratio see Intal and Llanto 1998, Table 5.

[170] Intal et al. 1998, 147.

[171] See Hutchcroft 1999.

ratio (close to 20 percent). However, the fact that these advantages were present does not rule out the possibility that bank capital was stringently regulated. Arguments that focus overwhelmingly on these advantages at the expense of the positive role played by supervisors do not give sufficient weight to the fact that, even with such advantages, regulators had to undertake significant regulatory efforts to avert a precipitous drop in the capital–asset *ratio* under liberal capital flows. I provide the somewhat technical rationale for this claim in the following paragraphs.

Capital flow liberalization contributed to a doubling of bank assets (the denominator of the capital–asset ratio) in the Philippines.[172] Estimates of nonperforming loans prior to the crisis average out at around 10 percent.[173] Given the sharp increase in assets (the denominator), a failure by regulators to substantially raise the banks' capital buffer *level* (the numerator) following liberalization would have left the capital–asset ratio below nonperforming loans. Philippine regulators, however, implemented increases in the numerator (the capital level) that were almost commensurate with the extreme jump in the denominator (assets). While the capital–asset–*ratio* fell below its inflated pre-liberalization level, these dramatic increases in capital *levels* ensured that nonperforming loans did not exceed the capital–asset ratio. This achievement is reflected in the fact that the Philippines rates well on the part of the World Bank's regulatory evaluation that focuses on bank capitalization (see Appendix 1).

This outcome with respect to capital is consistent with what this book predicts for an environment where a chief executive who does not have crony links to bank owners is free to appoint a trusted associate as a signaler of bank regulatory information, in an issue area that is not subject to legislative checks. Ramos did not have cronyistic links to the banking sector. Furthermore, Ramos was unobstructed from implementing a solution to the signaling problem, appointing a trusted childhood friend as central bank governor. Consistent with this arrangement, there is no evidence of signaling problems between Singson and Ramos. Finally, Ramos was not subject to gridlock when it came to enforcing a high capital–asset ratio because the new central bank was authorized to make this decision independently from the legislature. Thus, all the conditions conducive to

---

[172] See Intal and Llanto 1998, Table 1 for information on asset growth.

[173] Berg 1999 offers the highest estimate of 14 percent, but my interviews in the Philippines reveal a level of around 5 percent. 10 percent roughly falls between these estimates.

the stringent regulation of capital were present, and the outcome was accordingly good in this realm.

However, all this was not sufficient to generate a stringent regulatory environment overall. In realms of regulation where legislative approval was still required for the introduction of reforms, the Ramos government faced significant checks against moving toward a stringent environment. One of the realms of regulation in which the Philippines scores poorly relative to Hong Kong and Singapore is the capability of its legal system to enforce bank regulations. (See Appendix 1 for the components of the so-called CAMELOT ratings of bank regulatory environments.) The Philippine legal system generated exceptional enforcement difficulties for bank regulators, in that bankers were allowed to file personal lawsuits against regulators for taking regulatory actions against them. As Paul Hutchcroft puts it, "supervisors do indeed remain open to 'suits arising from the normal performance of duties' – that is, personally vulnerable for acts undertaken in an official capacity. Nonetheless Singson argues that officers and examiners are given greater protection [under the new central bank law] since their legal defense against lawsuits is assumed by the Monetary Board. Unfortunately, this provision is unlikely to provide much solace . . . [since] in the event that they are found guilty of negligence or misconduct (in courtrooms where their banker adversaries are likely to have much higher priced lawyers), BSP personnel must repay all legal expenses earlier advanced."[174] All this, of course, generates incentives for regulators to overlook infractions of the rules, thereby diluting the stringency of the regulatory environment. While there was much talk about passing a law that would protect regulators from lawsuits, the Ramos government was unable to make headway on this score. The obstacle came from legislators who were concerned about the misuse of power by regulators.

Another area of weakness was the quality of the management cadre of banks, which experts consider to be a critical aspect of the regulatory environment. (Where management is of high quality the burden on regulators to ensure that mistakes are not being made is much smaller.) Singapore and Hong Kong achieved high marks on this score because they allowed foreign banks and, by association, their highly trained management cadres liberal access to their economies. Ramos tried to dramatically open up the Philippine banking industry to foreign participation, an effort

---

[174] Hutchcroft 1998a, 211.

that, if successful, would have contributed to high marks on this aspect of the regulatory environment. However, the legislature, under pressure from the large domestic banks, substantially watered down Ramos' initial proposals.[175] The final law limited entry to ten foreign banks alone, which were furthermore subjected to severe limits on the number and locations of their branches.[176]

In sum, the Philippines failed to have a stringent bank regulatory environment despite the fact that two successive presidents did not have crony ties to bank owners. This failure is attributable initially to signaling and subsequently to gridlock problems. This is consistent with the argument of this book, which suggests that democracies are vulnerable to lax regulation even when their chief executive is not a crony capitalist.

---

[175] See Hutchcroft 1999 for a description of Ramos' efforts.
[176] Hutchcroft 1999, 170.

5

Unorthodox Solutions to the Signaling Problem

The Cases of Malaysia and Indonesia

The prediction of this book is that authoritarian environments are unlikely to be subject to either signaling or gridlock problems. Thus, unlike environments with even a moderate number of checks, we should generally observe outcomes that are consistent with the preferences of the chief executive. In this chapter I address the two countries where the chief executives adopted unorthodox solutions to the signaling problem following capital flow liberalization. In one case, the chief executive appointed a long-time friend from his home village to closely monitor the central bank and finance ministry from a special senior advisory position. In the other, the chief executive sidelined senior financial bureaucrats and instead relied on relatives and close cronies who owned banks as his primary source of information on the banking sector. In neither case is there evidence of signaling problems. The chief executives of both countries had close ties to the banking sector. The outcome, lax regulation, was in line with both chief executives' preferences.

5.1 MALAYSIA

In the years leading up to the Asian crisis, Malaysia was an authoritarian country where political power was largely concentrated in its prime minister, Mahathir Mohamad. In Section 5.1.1, I provide some background information on Malaysia's political and economic environment in the years leading up to the liberalization of capital inflows in 1990.[1] In

---

[1] Although the Malaysian government dismantled a substantial number of controls on capital flows in the early 1970s, it continued to exercise restraints on inflows of capital into banks till it opened an offshore center, much akin to Thailand's BIBF, on the island of Labuan in 1990. Bank Negara 1994, 32.

Section 5.1.2, I describe Prime Minister Mahathir's inner circle of banking advisors in the 1990s. In Section 5.1.3, I address the bank regulatory environment during this period.

5.1.1 Background: Malaysia Before 1990

To understand why and how Malaysia has increasingly become a country where power is highly concentrated in the prime minister, one has to consider the recent history of ethnic conflict in this nation. Malaysia is a multiethnic society, with approximately 60 percent of its population consisting of ethnic-Malays, 30 percent of ethnic-Chinese, and 10 percent of ethnic-Indians. Between independence, in 1957, and 1970, the nation's per-capita income rose by 25 percent. However ethnic-Malays, being largely concentrated in traditional rural occupations or in low-skilled jobs in the urban sector, were not among the significant beneficiaries of economic growth. By 1970, the per-capita income of ethnic-Malays amounted to only 57 percent of ethnic-Indian and 43 percent of ethnic-Chinese per-capita incomes.[2] These disparities gave rise to simmering tensions that finally came to a head following the 1969 national election.[3] Non-Malay ethnic groups made significant gains in this election, leading to substantial concerns on the part of ethnic-Malays about their future role in Malaysian political and economic life. Violent riots broke out, resulting in the deaths of hundreds of ethnic-Chinese.[4] These riots generated a concerted response on the part of the ethnic-Malay leadership, which had hitherto ruled the country in a consociational arrangement with other ethnic groups, to unilaterally remake the political institutions of the country.

Most significantly, the ruling ethnic-Malay party, the United Malays National Organization, created a political environment that presented severe constraints to opposition activity. I briefly describe these constraints, which persist to this day, as follows. One set of constraints goes by the moniker of the 3Ms – media, machinery, and money. Strict legislation restricts the media's freedom of expression. As Milne and Mauzy put it, "the constitution provides for freedom of speech, and of the media, but also stipulates that this freedom may be restricted by legislation in the interests of security or public order. The principal instrument used is the

---

[2] Crouch 1997, 21.
[3] Malaysia has a Westminster-type parliamentary system.
[4] Crouch 1997, 24.

Sedition Act, which prohibits comment on issues defined as sensitive."[5] In 1987, following a challenge to Prime Minister Mahathir Mohamad's rule from within the ruling party, the Sedition Act was amended and toughened, along with the Printing Presses and Publications Act. The consequence of these amendments is that the government has broad powers to ban or restrict publication.[6] (In 1987, three newspapers were banned for six months.)

Further contributing to the constraint on free expression is the tight control exerted over ownership of media outlets. As Milne and Mauzy put it, "control of the press is now almost entirely in the hands of the government or pro-government organizations. The English press and the Malay press are now almost entirely government owned."[7] The consequence is that the opposition, as well as challengers to the prime minister's rule from within his own party, seldom receive accurate or adequate coverage in the mainstream press, which substantially constrains their ability to court public opinion.

As far as the machinery component of the 3Ms is concerned, the machinery of government is often utilized to reinforce the reelection prospects of the incumbent. Most importantly, supposedly in order to avoid ethnic clashes, outdoor rallies have been banned in Malaysia since 1969. However, this ban does not prohibit government leaders from organizing gatherings related to government work, such as for opening new projects.[8] These gatherings are often used to make campaign speeches and deliver state largesse, which leaves the opposition at a distinct disadvantage.

As far as the money component is concerned, the distribution of state largesse has already been mentioned. In addition, the ban on outdoor rallies forces contenders to rely on expensive door-to-door campaigning at which the better financed ruling party has a distinct advantage because it can pay campaign workers better. In addition, "since the number of campaign posters and vehicles is not limited by law, this tends to benefit parties with greater access to funds."[9]

In addition to the 3Ms, Malaysia continues to have on its books an Internal Security Act that allows the government to make arrests without

---

[5] Milne and Mauzy 1999, 113.
[6] Milne and Mauzy 1999, 113.
[7] Milne and Mauzy 1999, 114.
[8] Gomez 2000, 266.
[9] Gomez 2000, 266.

charges being filed and without judicial review, all in the name of national security. In the decade prior to the currency crisis, this Act was most significantly used on two occasions. The first was in 1987, when several members of the opposition, including the prominent opposition leader Lim Kit Siang, were jailed for several months. The second was in 1990, when the brother of an opposition chief minister was detained.[10]

These features of the institutional environment exist against the backdrop of an electoral system that limits fragmentation of the vote. Since achieving independence from British colonial rule Malaysia has had a Westminster-type parliamentary system. Power rests in the *Dewan Rakyat* (House of Representatives), the members of which are elected from plurality-based single-member constituencies. The Upper House, which was originally intended to contribute to federalism, no longer plays such a role because the majority of its members are appointed by the federal government. In addition, while there is a constitutional monarch, a position that is held by one of the nine Malay former rulers of states for a five-year term, his discretionary powers are limited to "matters pertaining to Malay culture and tradition."[11]

In keeping with what we should expect from a Westminster-type system, Malaysia's electoral system provides the prime minister with a clear majority. This has been the case despite the many ethnic divisions, and associated political allegiances, in this country. The ethnic-Malay United Malays National Organization (UMNO), which has led every government since independence, has seen fit to include Chinese and Indian parties and rule in a coalition. However, the coalitional or consociational aspects of this arrangement have primarily been of symbolic value in the last two decades; the coalition, known as the *Barisan Nasional* (BN), has been heavily dominated by its leader. As Edmund Terrence Gomez points out, "UMNO leaders have openly asserted that the party could rule alone, but prefers to share power in the interest of national unity."[12] In effect, this power-sharing arrangement has consisted of "accommodation on Malay terms," leading most analysts to argue that Malaysia's political system is dominated by one party, UMNO.[13]

Further contributing to the concentration of power in Malaysia is the fact that, with rare exceptions, party discipline is exceptionally strong.

---

[10] Milne and Mauzy 1999, 106–109.
[11] Gomez 2000, 226.
[12] Gomez 2000, 272.
[13] Gomez 2000, 271.

The prime minister is the key player in allocating parliamentary seats between UMNO party members as well as coalition partners, and has considerable command over patronage resources. Consequently, "Barisan Nasional parliamentarians usually endorse new legislation and policies, customarily with minimal or no protests."[14]

All of this results in a political system where an exceptional amount of power is concentrated in the prime minister. Given all of the above, we should expect policy outcomes to largely reflect the policy preferences of the prime minister in Malaysia. The question then is, what were these preferences?

Prime Minister Mahathir was no opponent of cronyism, especially when it came to supporting ethnic-Malay businesspeople who were close to the ruling party. Under Mahathir, the Malaysian government embarked on a massive program of privatization aimed at increasing the participation of ethnic-Malay (*bumiputra*) businesspeople in the modern economy. However, he did not opt to conduct privatization in a transparent manner. As Gomez and Jomo put it, "it appears . . . that this ethnic agenda has served as a smokescreen which has obscured significant private accumulation by the politically well connected. . . . Privatization, part of Malaysia's liberalization package, has been especially abused for the consolidation and development of politically connected businessmen."[15] To support this claim, Gomez and Jomo have meticulously documented how privatization under Mahathir benefited cronies of the prime minister and his close advisors.[16]

Mahathir's inclination for ethnic cronyism is of special significance for bank regulation because it extended to restructuring the ownership of the banking sector. Several banks that were owned by businesspeople without close government ties were turned over to the control of the government and favored ethnic-Malay businesspeople. As Gomez and Jomo point out, by the 1990s, "eight of the top ten local banks, once primarily dominated by Chinese and foreign interests, were brought under the control of *Bumiputera* [ethnic-Malay] and government companies."[17] If Mahathir's affirmative action programs generated a set of lenders with whom he had close ties, it also generated a set of borrowers with dubious

---

[14] Gomez 2000, 275.
[15] Gomez and Jomo 1997, 179.
[16] Gomez and Jomo 1997.
[17] Gomez and Jomo 1997, 62.

credentials who were closely connected to him. Gomez and Jomo point out that "most politically connected businessmen have tended to concentrate their rent-appropriating activities in the relatively protected import-substituting manufacturing, services, and other non-tradeables [sectors] such as real property construction and infrastructure, while others have gained mostly from often complex paper shuffling, asset stripping and other similar corporate manoevres, rather than from significant gains in productivity or in international competitiveness."[18]

In sum, Malaysia had a prime minister with close cronyistic ties to bank owners in an authoritarian environment. As per the theory of this book, we should not expect the bank regulatory environment to be stringent under such conditions. Indeed, the Mahathir government's record prior to the 1990s was more one of reforms following major crises than of stringent *ex ante* regulation to prevent crises from happening in the first place.

In 1983, the Hong Kong–based subsidiary of the state-owned Bank Bumiputra collapsed, primarily on account of its excessive exposure to one firm (BMF) owned by a businessman with close ties to UMNO.[19] In response, the government was forced to pump in funds from the state-owned petroleum company, Petronas, to replenish the bank's shareholder capital base. The loss to the government amounted to RM 2.5 billion. As Natasha Hamilton-Hart has pointed out, there were several regulatory failures associated with this collapse. Irregularities in the transfer of funds to BMF were ignored, auditors' reports of overexposure to BMF were disregarded, and action to remove the directors of BMF and Bank Bumiputra was delayed. In Hamilton-Hart's words, "overall the BMF affair was consistent with a pattern of permissiveness by the central bank when interests close to leading politicians was involved . . . open personal enrichment did not provoke countermeasures until the failure of the project (and the costs this would impose on the state) were well in the open."[20]

The banking sector experienced further stress in the mid-1980s, when several institutions proved to be insufficiently robust to withstand a severe recession.[21] As R. Thillainathan succinctly describes it, the recession "was

---

[18] Gomez and Jomo 1997, 179.
[19] Milne and Mauzy 1999, 69.
[20] Hamilton-Hart 2002, 121.
[21] Thillainathan 1998, 3.

on account of austerity policies forced on the government by mounting domestic and external debts, collapse of key commodity prices (with the terms of trade worsening on an average by 10% p.a. over the two years), very tight monetary policy (with base money growing at 4% p.a. over 1983 to 1987), an over valued exchange rate in the early and mid-1980s (caused by a desire to maintain a parity of the Malaysian ringgit vis-à-vis the Singapore dollar, excessive external borrowings and increased export earnings from oil and gas) and stifling pro-distribution policies. GNP declined... sharply in money terms at 5% p.a. in 1985 and 1986 (vs. a growth rate of 10.9% over the preceding five years)."[22]

The stress experienced by the banking sector during the recession was partly on account of overexposure to some critical groups of borrowers. In particular, "those who had built up their gross assets through speculation in shares and property, financed through excessive gearing, were caught in a triple squeeze: they faced a sharp decline in income flows, a collapse in asset values, and a rise in the cost of debt service."[23] The four banks that were most in need of rehabilitation were all affected "mainly by heavy losses from their involvement in the property sector."[24] Significantly, the share of the property sector in total loans had risen from 26.4 percent in 1980 to 35.9 percent by 1986.[25] As a share of new loans the share of this sector had actually jumped from 30 percent in 1980 and 32 percent in 1983 to 55 percent in 1986, thanks in particular to speculative loans for high-rise commercial buildings.[26] Partly as a consequence of these increases, nonperforming loans rose to as high as 30 percent in 1988.[27]

The severity of the shock to the banking sector arguably generated a sense of caution on Mahathir's part with respect to the banking sector, which partially alleviated the powerfully cronyistic tendencies that were inherent in his close ties to the banking sector, which were described previously. The most significant response of Mahathir's government to the stress of the 1980s was to embark on efforts to enforce a high capital asset ratio. (By 1990, the central bank was already enforcing a ratio of

---

[22] Thillainathan 1998, 3.
[23] Sheng 1996, 113.
[24] Sheng 1996, 115.
[25] Thillainathan 1998, 4.
[26] Looi 1987, 41 and 50.
[27] Bank Negara 1997, 138.

10 percent, versus 6 percent prior to the recession.)[28] However, the fact that the shock did not go so far as to result in a preference for stringent regulation on Mahathir's part can be seen from the fact that no regulatory measures were undertaken to avert the recurrence of the phenomenon of overexposure to the property sector, where, as mentioned, cronies were well represented.

In response to the 1980s crisis, the government also replaced the boards of directors of some banks, increased on-site examinations of banks' accounts, and strengthened the powers of regulators to prevent financial institutions from accepting new deposits and to take over institutions that had engaged in dubious lending practices.[29] However, cronyism played an important part even in these reforms. Three banks were singled out to find new investors; all three were foreign-owned banks. Meanwhile, some equally weak banks that were owned by locals were spared such drastic action, and some entered the 1990s in a weak condition.[30]

In Malaysia, the central bank governor is subordinate to the finance minister. In none of the turmoil in the 1980s is there any indication of signaling problems between the finance minister and the prime minister. This is not surprising, because the finance minister for most of the 1980s was Daim Zainuddin. Daim, who was born in the same *kampong* (village) as Prime Minister Mahathir, was one of Mahathir's oldest and closest associates.[31] Daim spearheaded Mahathir's privatization plan and was an active proponent of handing out particularistic benefits to ethnic-Malay businesspeople. As Asiamoney points out, "Daim Zainuddin . . . reshaped the Malaysian economy, diffusing the control of Chinese entrepreneurs by hand-picking bumiputras [ethnic-Malays] to run businesses in many of the key sectors."[32] His close ties to these businessmen are estimated to have yielded him a net worth of $200 to 500 million.[33]

With Daim operating as finance minister, Mahathir was clearly operating with an official who closely shared his priorities. It thus stands to reason that there is no evidence of signaling problems between Daim and Mahathir serving as an obstacle to Mahathir implementing his policy preferences.

---

[28] Bank Negara 1994, 144.
[29] Sheng 1996, 117.
[30] Delhaise 1998, 147.
[31] Milne and Mauzy 1999, 70.
[32] Asiamoney May 1996, 34.
[33] Milne and Mauzy 1999, 71.

5.1.2 The Inner Circle of Banking Advisors

In 1990, when the inauguration of an offshore financial center at Labuan liberalized capital inflows into banks, Daim was still the finance minister. In 1991, Anwar Ibrahim took Daim's place. This shift was, to some degree, forced upon Mahathir by Anwar's emergence as a credible heir apparent. However, Anwar's ascension did not mean that Mahathir was significantly distanced from the finance ministry. This was the case because Mahathir, operating in an authoritarian environment, had recourse to a highly unorthodox solution. Mahathir created an ad hoc position for Daim with wide-ranging powers that often superceded those of the finance minister. This included the power to observe all financial data that was confidential to the government. In effect, Mahathir ensured that an official who shared his preferences would continue to have access to private information on the financial sector, via an unorthodox solution to the signaling problem.

Indeed, Daim's continued participation as an alternative power center for financial decision-making was a source of immense discomfort to Anwar. For instance, there were differences between Anwar and Daim over a megaproject, called the Bakun Dam project, which was the source of major rents for ethnic-Malays closely connected with Daim.[34] Anwar was also involved in a dispute with Daim over the privatization of shares in a major bank. As Gomez and Jomo describe this dispute, "Anwar was ... believed to have been upset over reports that at least 60% of the government owned Bank Bumiputra's equity was to have been bought over, without his consent, by Samsuddin Hasan, a protégé of Daim; this appeared to challenge Anwar's power over his own domain, the Finance Ministry."[35]

From the above it is apparent that Daim's departure from the finance ministership by no means went with his departure from Mahathir's inner circle. This squares well with the absence of evidence that Mahathir was in any way ill informed about the state of the banking sector after Anwar became finance minister. It is plausible to conclude that Mahathir retained Daim in his inner circle precisely because he did not entirely trust Anwar. Future events would appear to justify such a decision. Once the Asian crisis struck, Anwar, in opposition to Mahathir, came out as a supporter of an IMF-style adjustment regime that would have severely affected the

---

[34] Milne and Mauzy 1999, 148.
[35] Gomez and Jomo 1997, 112.

fortunes of several of Mahathir's cronies. This suggests that if Mahathir had relied exclusively on Anwar as a signaler, there would have been signaling problems on account of differing preferences. The key point here, however, is that in an environment with very few checks on his power, Mahathir was not obliged to rely on an official with different preferences for his signals. In the absence of significant checks, he was free to appoint a trusted crony to observe financial information and create a congenial signaling environment, which is what the theory predicts.

With Daim operating as advisor at large with access to private government information, Mahathir was not forced to rely on the central bank governor either for signals. For the record, neither Jaffar Hussain, who served as governor in the early years after liberalization, nor Ahmad Don, who replaced him in 1994, was considered to be a cronyistic official. However, with Daim serving as a trusted signaler, the preferences of these officials were rendered irrelevant from a signaling perspective. (Recall that just one signaler with shared preferences is sufficient to solve the signaling problem.) Consistent with the resort to an unorthodox solution to the signaling problem, there is no evidence that Mahathir was, at any point, misinformed about the true state of the banking sector.

5.1.3 The Bank Regulatory Environment in the 1990s

While there is no evidence of gridlock or signaling problems, Malaysia's bank regulatory environment exhibited several major weaknesses that can be attributed to Mahathir's cronyistic preferences. One major area where Malaysia appeared to perform well was with respect to the capital–asset ratio. Recall that Malaysia's primary response to its banking crisis of the 1980s was to raise the minimum ratio of capital to assets that banks were expected to maintain. Recall also that regulators were enforcing a ratio of capital to assets of 10 percent by 1990. In 1993, the year in which capital inflows were at their highest, all merchant banks and finance companies were in compliance with the capital–asset ratio rule, and only three commercial banks out of twenty-two fell below the required minimum.[36] At the time of the Asian crisis, capital–asset ratios ranged from 8 to 14 percent, with an average of 12 percent.[37]

Although capital–asset ratios were relatively high, Malaysia's banking regulatory environment still cannot be called stringent. Recall from the

[36] Bank Negara 1994, 144.
[37] Corsetti et al. 1998.

model in Chapter 3 that, even when the capital–asset ratio is high, a banking sector will not be robust if it carries a large quantity of loans that are vulnerable to default. This was the case in Malaysia.

As the Malaysian economy became a major recipient of international capital flows, an asset bubble began to emerge in the property sector as well as in the stock market on account of heavy bank lending to these sectors. House prices jumped by 29 percent in Kuala Lumpur in 1995.[38] There was an increase in condominium building of 86 percent in 1994, followed by 53 percent in 1995.[39] Lending to the property sector increased at a rate of close to 30 percent through 1996, until loans to this sector came to amount to 45 percent of total bank credit.[40] As far as the bubble in the stock market is concerned, Philippe Delhaise characterizes this market as "a giant casino making up for very restrictive laws on gambling."[41] Bank exposure to the stock market jumped by 31 percent in 1996 alone.[42] The presence of an asset bubble is, of course, associated with exceptionally high expected defaults, which means that, despite having a relatively high capital–asset ratio, the Malaysian banking sector fell short of being moderately robust.

That Mahathir would choose to barely regulate property and stock market lending is entirely consistent with his crony ties. Recall that, following Mahathir's privatization program, the property and financial sectors became heavily populated with Mahathir's protégés. As Malaysian economist Prema Chandra Athukorala has pointed out, heavy lending to these sectors was in all likelihood driven by Mahathir's priority of supporting the financial interests of these protégés.[43]

In sum, there is no evidence of signaling or gridlock problems, and the stringency of the regulatory environment in Malaysia was consistent with the preferences of its chief executive, which is what the theory predicts for authoritarian environments.

5.2 INDONESIA

For three decades preceding the Asian currency crisis, Indonesia was governed by a military regime called the "New Order," led by President

---

[38] Bank Negara 1997b, 101.
[39] Bank Negara 1997b, 101.
[40] Ariff et al. 1998, 7, and Athukorala 1998, 92.
[41] Delhaise 1998, 149.
[42] Bank Negara 1997b, 71.
[43] Athukorala 1998, 93.

Soeharto. In Section 5.2.1, I describe the concentration of power in the presidency under the New Order. Section 5.2.2 addresses the Soeharto regime's governance record prior to liberalizing controls on capital inflows into banks in 1989.[44] I demonstrate that there was a sharp difference in the Soeharto regime's governance performance between macro- and micro-economic policy realms. In Section 5.2.3, I describe Soeharto's inner circle of banking advisors in the 1990s. In Section 5.2.4, I describe how bank regulations were enforced during this period.

5.2.1   The Political Environment Under the New Order

Although the New Order allowed for periodic elections, there were several factors that undermined their competitiveness. Most importantly, the president was elected by a People's Consultative Assembly, which consisted of 1000 members, half of which came from the House of Representatives and the rest of which were appointed by the president. Given that the president appointed 20 percent of the members of the House from the Army, the president effectively appointed 60 percent of the Consultative Assembly. The whole exercise de facto amounted to the president appointing himself to repeated five-year terms.[45]

While a large proportion of the House of Representatives consisted of elected representatives, there were several factors that undermined the competitiveness of elections, rendering Indonesia under Soeharto an authoritarian state. Andrew MacIntyre has recently offered a comprehensive analysis of these factors.[46]

First, the government tightly controlled the entry and exit of political parties into/from the political arena. As far as entry controls were concerned, "primarily on the basis of official statute but periodically with recourse to unofficial inducement and coercion as well, the government [was] able to determine whether a party may contest an election, whether an individual may stand for election as the representative of a party, and which individuals may serve as leaders of the parties."[47] With regard to exit, the government had the power to dissolve any party whose ideology

---

[44] Capital outflows had been liberalized as early as 1970, but limits on capital inflows into banks remained in place till May 1989. See Cole and Slade 1996, xxv and 115.

[45] MacIntyre 1999a, 267.

[46] MacIntyre 1999a.

[47] MacIntyre 1999a, 262.

was not considered compatible with state goals, which were defined by the president.

Second, the government put powerful pressure on all government employees to join the government's party, *Golkar*. Civil servants were automatically enrolled as members of the Indonesian Civil Servants Corp (KOPRI), which had a corporatist link to *Golkar*. In addition, civil servants had to have permission from their superiors to join any other party, which was not likely to be granted. Further limiting the freedom for maneuver for civil servants, senior officials were often called upon to canvass support for the ruling party prior to elections.[48]

Third, laws on the books prevented political parties from establishing branches at the village level. As MacIntyre puts it, "this restriction has proved a powerful advantage to Golkar since, even though it may not set up party branches in villages, it is able to run *de facto* campaigns at this level because because local officials such as the village head or local police officer or representative of the armed forces are all civil servants responsible to the national government, and are thus almost certain to be Golkar members and subject to informal incentives to rally support for Golkar at election times."[49]

Fourth, the government had unequal access to the media, on account of its willingness to ban publications that published inconvenient facts, state-owned television's obvious bias, and tight control of the licensing of private television channels that kept them exclusively in the hands of *Golkar* sympathizers.[50]

In sum, the New Order regime was one where power was heavily concentrated in one actor, President Soeharto. Soeharto's assumption of power was significantly precipitated by the macroeconomic chaos inflicted by his predecessor, Sukarno, on the Indonesian economy. This played an important role in creating a sharp bifurcation between macro- and microeconomic policy realms in the New Order, which I describe in the next section.

5.2.2 *Economic Governance Prior to 1990*

Under Sukarno, the Indonesian government ran massive fiscal deficits to the point that that government revenues did not even cover salary

---

[48] MacIntyre 1999a, 264.
[49] MacIntyre 1999a, 264.
[50] MacIntyre 1999a, 266.

expenditures. Sukarno ordered the central bank to inflate the money supply to cover the fiscal deficits. In 1965 alone, thanks to a fivefold increase in money supply and a budget deficit of 300 percent, inflation exceeded 500 percent after already having doubled in every year since 1961.[51] In sum, thanks to gross macroeconomic mismanagement, Indonesia's economy fell into virtual stagnation under Sukarno, contributing to his ouster.

Given the role of macroeconomic mismanagement in the displacement of his predecessor, it was apparent to Soeharto that, aside from retaining his firm grasp on the military, his hold on office was contingent on adhering to sound neo-classically conservative macroeconomic policies. Thus, Soeharto entrusted macroeconomic policy to economists centered around the University of Indonesia, led by the venerable Widjojo Nidisastro and four colleagues, who shared a firm belief in balanced budgets and conservative monetary policies.[52]

While Indonesia's economic recovery under Soeharto was considerably helped along by large quantities of foreign aid, generated by Cold War considerations, its macroeconomic performance was impressive by developing country standards. As the World Bank put it in its East Asian Miracle report, "the level of the [fiscal] deficit that is affordable, and hence not destabilizing is specific to each economy. It is generally larger the faster the rate of growth and the larger the pool of private savings (both home and abroad) relative to private investment. In both these dimensions, the High Performing Asian Economies [including Indonesia] have performed better than many of their developing country counterparts during the past thirty years. Because of this, while some economies have had higher inflation than others, none has had to endure the very high, debilitating inflation that has troubled other developing economies."[53] Indeed, Indonesia's average inflation rate of 12.8 percent between 1969 and 1991, compared to 61.8 percent for all low- and middle-income countries, confirms this view.[54]

Soeharto also received high praise from the World Bank for allowing his technocrats to adopt an orthodox macroeconomic response to the decline in oil prices between 1982 and 1986.[55] As the World Bank

---

[51] Bresnan 1993, 54–57.
[52] The four remaining economists were Mohammad Sadli, Emil Salim, Subroto, and Ali Wardhana. Bresnan 1993, 64.
[53] World Bank 1993, 107.
[54] World Bank 1993, 110.
[55] Indonesia is a major oil exporter.

describes it, "starting in 1983 the government responded with a remarkably comprehensive and successful adjustment program. It devalued the *rupiah* in 1983 and 1986 and cut expenditures, mainly by rescheduling capital-intensive projects. The need to reduce the current account deficit without creating a recession was straightforward; the orthodox solutions were effective. A measure of the achievement from 1985 is illustrated by the following calculation. The excess of imports of goods and non-factor services over non-oil exports fell from 15% of GDP in 1984 to 7% in 1988. This shift of 8% of GDP measures the extent to which absorption had to be reduced – the effects of increased payments of long term debt, higher interest payments, and reduced income from oil and gas imports. This massive resource shift, also associated with trade liberalization, was brought about without increased inflation."[56]

However, Soeharto's preferences on microeconomic policy, of which bank regulation is a part, were another story altogether. Since relatively early in his career, Soeharto had displayed a willingness to collaborate with Indonesia's Chinese-Indonesian business community in mutually profitable ventures. (While serving as a commander in Diponegoro, Soeharto had been sanctioned by the military for corruption.[57]) Soeharto had free rein to act on this preference in the microeconomic realm after he became the sole veto player.

As far as banking is concerned, until the late 1980s, state-owned banks contributed to 70 percent of the assets of the banking sector. Indonesia's state-owned banks were best known for directing massive quantities of loans to businessmen who were close to Soeharto, which had very weak prospects for being repaid.[58] The banking sector was thus not close to being robust, but this, far from being the result of lack of information or miscalculation, was precisely because Soeharto wanted to use the state banks as a massive source of patronage. Support for this view comes from the fact that using the state banks in this way was entirely consistent with Soeharto's record of particularism in other realms of microeconomic policy. I offer a few representative examples in the following paragraphs.

Soeharto granted his family members lucrative distribution contracts for the products of the state-owned oil company, Pertamina. As Adam Schwartz points out, such contracts generated hundreds of millions

---

[56] World Bank 1993, 118–119.
[57] Bresnan 1993, 46.
[58] Schwartz 1994, 151 and Cole and Slade 1996, 139.

of dollars in middleman revenues that could have been kept by the state.[59] Furthermore, Soeharto granted his family members an exclusive license for the import of plastic. This enterprise added 10–15 percent to the price of plastic and netted Soeharto's family members $30 million in profits in 1986 alone.[60] In addition, Soeharto granted his son Tommy a soybean crushing monopoly, his half-brother Probosutedjo and Chinese-Indonesian businessman Liem Sieoe Long a clove-importing monopoly, and cousin Sudwikatmono a motion picture importing monopoly.[61]

In addition, Soeharto placed the prominent Chinese-Indonesian businessman Bob Hasan in control of the Indonesian Plywood Association, the Indonesian Sawmillers Association, the Indonesian Ratan Association, and the umbrella Indonesian Forestry Community.[62] Hasan won Soeharto's support, over the objections of the forestry bureaucracy, to engage in the overharvesting of forests and the skimming of reforestation funds.[63]

Furthermore, Soeharto allowed businessmen cronies to establish monopolies on the sale of urea fertilizer tablets and tin-plate imports. As Michael Backman puts it, "many [of these] ventures involved securing licenses and distribution rights that simply pushed up prices and penalized ordinary Indonesians.... Bureaucrats were routinely pressurized into signing [these] contracts, even when the deal was not in their particular agency's best interest."[64]

5.2.3 The Inner Circle of Banking Advisors from 1989 to 1997

In 1989, when capital flows into banks were liberalized, the central bank governor and the finance ministers were, respectively, Adrianus Mooy and Johannes Sumarlin. In 1993, Mooy and Sumarlin were replaced by Soedradjad Djiwandono and Mar'ie Muhammad. Of these officials, the latter two, at least, were not considered to be cronies. (The appointment of noncrony officials was, in all likelihood, aimed at impressing international donors, who contributed massively to Indonesia's economy.) However, the business connections and preferences of all these officials were moot from a signaling perspective. Important liberalization reforms in banking were

---

[59] Schwartz 1994, 139.
[60] Backman 1999, 267.
[61] Backman 1999, 267.
[62] Schwartz 1994, 139–140.
[63] Schwartz 1994, 140.
[64] Backman 1999, 273–274.

Table 5.1 *Number of Banks in Indonesia*

	1987	1988	1989	1990	1991	1992	1993	1994
State banks	7	7	7	7	7	7	7	7
Private banks	64	63	88	106	126	141	158	166
Foreign and joint venture	11	11	23	28	39	30	39	40
Regional development banks	27	27	27	27	27	27	27	27
TOTAL	109	108	145	168	199	205	231	240

Source: Cole and Slade 1996, 114.

managed in a fashion that resulted in Soeharto having a direct view of the state of the banking sector from his relatives and close friends, without any intermediation from the above officials.

Private participation in the Indonesian banking sector was dramatically liberalized in the 1980s. In these liberalization reforms, private commercial banks were only required to put up $5.8 million in initial capital in order to receive a license. As Cole and Slade put it, "there was a popular belief that the relatively easy approval and low capital requirements for new banks would not last indefinitely and it was advisable to apply quickly before the rules were again tightened."[65] The consequence was an explosion in the number of banks. In one year alone the number of private banks increased by twenty-five, which is the total number of domestically owned banks in the Malaysian banking sector and one-half the number of banks in the Philippine banking sector. Table 5.1 shows the dramatic increase in private participation in the Indonesian banking sector after the late 1980s.

In addition to the increase in the number of institutions, the share of private banks in total lending grew from less than one-quarter to over 40 percent of all lending in five years (see Table 5.2).

Many of Soeharto's cronies, as well as family members, participated aggressively in this expansion of the banking sector. For instance, the major shareholder of Indonesia's largest bank (Bank Central Asia) was Soeharto's long-standing business associate Liem Sioe Long

---

[65] Cole and Slade 1996, 114.

Table 5.2 *Bank Assets by Ownership Group in Indonesia*
(Percent of Total Banking Sector Assets)

	State	Private Domestic	Regional Development	Foreign and Joint Venture
1988	67	24	4	5
1989	59	32	4	6
1990	54	36	3	7
1991	51	38	4	8
1992	52	36	3	8
1993	49	41	3	8
1994	43	43	4	9

Source: Cole and Slade 1996, 108.

(70%).[66] Soeharto's daughter, Siti Hardijanti Rukmana (known as "Tutut") owned 14 percent of this bank and her brother, Sigit Harjojudanto, owned the remaining 16 percent. Sigit also owned a medium-sized bank in partnership with his younger brother, Tommy. Liem, in partnership with another close Soeharto associate, Prajogo Pangestu, also had a controlling share in the prominent Bank Summa. Prajogo also owned a small bank, Bank Andromeda, in partnership with Soeharto's second son, Bambang. Bob Hasan, who was Sigit's business partner, also had substantial interests in the banking sector.[67]

The rich web of partnerships between prominent Chinese-Indonesian businessmen and Soeharto's family in banking was just the tip of the iceberg with respect to the many joint ventures between these groups.[68] As these ventures proliferated in the 1990s, Soeharto's preferences became even more perfectly aligned with those of the crony private business groups, and he began to rely even more on the advice of his cronies prior to making microeconomic decisions. Soeharto began to unceremoniously sideline senior bureaucrats from the decision-making process. As Adam Schwartz quotes a prominent technocrat, "there is no question that

---

[66] By 1997 Bank Central Asia had overtaken the state owned Bank BNI as the country's largest bank. In addition, the privately owned Bank Danamon, Bank Dagang Nasional Indonesia, and Bank Internasional Indonesia were only slightly smaller than Bank BNI by this point.

[67] *FEER* June 4, 1998, 68; *Asiaweek* June 5, 1998, 37; Schwartz 1994, 110,140,143, 151; and Backman 1999, 97.

[68] See Backman 1999 for a listing of these ventures.

Soeharto listens more to Liem and Prajogo and Hasan and his children now compared to five or even two years ago. He seems to think that these business practitioners are giving him better advice than the economists."[69]

For Soeharto to rely on relatives and friends in the banking sector who shared his cronyistic preferences for advice, rather than on noncrony bureaucrats like Soedradjad, of course falls in the category of finding an unorthodox solution to the signaling problem. In an environment with few checks, there was nothing to stop Soeharto from relegating senior financial bureaucrats to the sidelines while promoting cronies to perform the main signaling role. Given that there is no evidence of legislative gridlock in Indonesia under Soeharto's authoritarian rule, as we should expect, the critical question remaining is, what exactly were Soeharto's and his cronies' preferences in the realm of banking?

Soeharto's and the cronies' priorities amounted to a preference for a fragile banking sector kept afloat primarily by the implicit promise of government bailouts. The favored form of fragility of the Indonesian banking sector had a distinctive character. Heavy lending by banks to their owners, to the point that it exceeds bank capital, is tantamount to having bank owners inject negative capital into their banks. Crony businesspeople entered the Indonesian banking sector precisely to engage in such lending; as Michael Backman, a keen observer of Indonesian banking practices, puts it, "many Indonesian conglomerates established their own bank for no other reason than to act as the banker to the group."[70] As one bank director put it to Backman, "we own a bank because what is the point of giving others the spread [between the interest rate paid to depositors and the lending rate]. . . . Our chairman thinks that there is no sense in one division borrowing while the other has deposits."[71] As Philippe Delhaise humorously puts it, "Indonesia's bankers are Asia's most skilled related party lenders. It is a national pastime, which is not surprising when most banks belong to families or to industrial or commercial groups."[72] The emphasis on this form of connected lending meant that Indonesian bankers and their patron, Soeharto, effectively had a preference for injecting minimal capital into banks, irrespective of expected defaults, after taking lending to bank shareholders into account. This meant that their ideal point on banking sector robustness was far left

---

[69] Quoted in Schwartz 1994, 159.
[70] Backman 2000, 86.
[71] Backman 2000, 85.
[72] Delhaise 1998, 130.

of the center of the robustness continuum. In the next section, I show that the robustness outcome and the stringency of the regulatory environment were in line with these preferences, just as we should expect in an authoritarian environment.

5.2.4 *The Bank Regulatory Environment in the 1990s*

The finance ministry and the central bank introduced new rules governing the regulation of banks in February 1991 and subsequently in March 1992. The former set of regulations called for all banks to raise their ratio of capital to assets to 5 percent by April 1992, 7 percent by March of 1993, and to be in full compliance with the Bank for International Settlements' recommended ratio (8%) by the end of 1993. In addition, the banks were banned from owning equity securities or financing trade in stocks and securities. Stringent legal limits were also placed on banks' open foreign exchange positions.[73]

A critical aspect of the second set of regulations, which were included in the Banking Law of 1992, was new rules aimed at restricting lending by banks to affiliated companies. Loans by banks to a single borrower were limited to less than 20 percent of bank capital. The limit on loans to affiliated borrowers and shareholders was set at 30 and 5 percent, respectively.[74]

The introduction of the latter set of rules was crucial to ensure de facto compliance with the international capital–asset ratio norm introduced earlier, because an 8 percent ratio is only considered acceptable assuming that bank loan portfolios are not heavily skewed toward affiliated parties. As mentioned earlier, this is the case because heavy affiliated party lending means that bank owners in fact owe their banks money beyond their original investment, which implies that they de facto have injected negative capital into the bank to serve as a buffer against expected defaults.[75]

As far as the enforcement record is concerned, while less than 10 percent of the banks failed to meet the 8 percent capital–asset ratio requirement, this record of enforcement was rendered moot by the massive expansion in affiliated party lending in the mid-1990s.[76] The proportion of banks that were in violation of affiliated party lending limits jumped

---

[73] Cole and Slade 1996, 93.
[74] Cole and Slade 1996, 133.
[75] Delhaise 1998, 130.
[76] Bank Indonesia 1997, 73.

from 15 percent in 1994 to 33 percent in 1995, and remained at this level in 1996–97.[77] As David Cole and Betty Slade put it, "any financial regulator who attempted to apply prudential rules to connected financial institutions or transactions, for example Bank Indonesia Managing Director Binhadi in 1992, or Director General Martiono from the Ministry of Finance in 1996, was removed from his position."[78]

In sum, consistent with the presence of the unorthodox solution, there is no evidence of signaling problems in Indonesia, and the laxness of the prudential regulatory environment was entirely consistent with Soeharto's preferences, as the theory predicts.

---

[77] Backman 1999, 73, and 86.
[78] Cole and Slade 1998, 65.

6

Orthodox Solutions to the Signaling Problem

The Cases of Singapore and Hong Kong

In this chapter, I address the two authoritarian countries where chief executives adopted the orthodox solution to the signaling problem, namely, to appoint close associates who shared their preferences to key bureaucratic positions. In both cases, the regulatory outcomes were in line with the chief executives' preferences for stringent regulation.

6.1 SINGAPORE

Recall that an authoritarian country whose chief executive has arm's length relations with the banking sector is predicted to have a stringent bank regulatory environment, unimpeded by signaling problems or gridlock. I show in this chapter that, although Singapore changed its development strategy several times in the course of the last three decades, there was one constant: arm's length relations between the chief executive and the entire business community, including the banking sector. I begin with a background section that addresses the period between 1965 and 1990, when Lee Kwan Yew served as the chief executive. In Section 6.2, I describe the political environment under Lee's successor, Goh Chok Tong. In Section 6.3, I describe the bank regulatory environment in Singapore in the years leading up to the Asian crisis.

6.1.1 Background: Singapore Between 1965 and 1990

Ever since its emergence as an independent state, Singapore has operated under a system of government that falls well short of being a democracy. The government's powers include detention without trial, deregistration and replacement of radical unions with compliant ones, and withdrawal

113

of licenses from newspapers deemed to be opposed to national interests.[1] In addition, there is a Societies Act that bars voluntary associations from making statements in sympathy with other associations. As Chua Beng-Huat has pointed out, "this effectively suppresses the commonplace activity of a civil society where voluntary associations establish their solidarity by publicly sympathizing with each others' causes."[2] Furthermore, members of opposition parties have often been persecuted by the government, via defamation proceedings or charges of tax evasion.[3]

The executive is headed by a prime minister, who is the leader of the party that holds the majority in Singapore's unicameral parliament.[4] While shares of the popular vote have varied from election to election, the People's Action Party (PAP) has always commanded an overwhelming majority of parliamentary seats. As Chua Beng-Huat points out, "the style of government is totally top down," with a firm insistence on party discipline within the PAP.[5]

From the time of its separation from Malaysia in 1965 until 1990, Singapore had a single prime minister, Lee Kwan Yew. Under Lee Singapore became one of the fastest growing economies in the world, growing at close to 7 percent per annum in the 1970s and at close to 6 percent per annum in the 1980s.[6] Singapore's remarkable economic record has been widely attributed to the government's success in flexibly adapting to the exigencies of the international marketplace to retain Singapore's appeal as a destination for international capital.[7] The government engineered three major strategy changes since independence in service of this goal. Underpinning each of these strategies, however, were "clean," arm's length relations between the government and business. I outline each of these strategy shifts in the following, demonstrating precisely how arm's length relations underpinned all the strategies.

Prior to 1965, Singapore's economy had long primarily relied on offering transshipment services for goods. However, independence from Malaysia forced the PAP government to reconsider its economic strategy.

---

[1] Beng-Huat 2001, 266.
[2] Beng-Huat 2001, 268.
[3] Beng-Huat 2001, 271.
[4] Till the reforms of 1991, and subsequent direct elections in 1993, the president was elected by the parliament and had a largely ceremonial role. I describe these reforms in the next section, which is devoted to the 1990s.
[5] Beng-Huat 2001, 268.
[6] Huff 1994, 352.
[7] See, for instance, Haggard 1990 and World Bank 1993.

Separation from Malaysia left Singapore without a substantial industrial base, and the entrepot trade could not be counted on to generate adequate employment. Concerns about employment were only heightened when the British government announced that it would withdraw all military forces by 1971, a decision that would result in the loss of 40,000 jobs.[8] One possible response to these problems that was followed in many other parts of the world would have been to adopt a strategy of import substitution. However, as Stephan Haggard points out, "with Singapore cut off from Malaysian markets, import substitution was not a viable strategy."[9] Furthermore, relying on local firms for export-led industrialization was not a viable option because local firms were heavily concentrated in real estate and domestic trade and thus had little experience or technological capability in manufacturing. The decision was thus made to compete for foreign investment in labor-intensive manufacturing for exports to the developed world.[10]

As part of the transition to this new growth strategy, earlier laws regulating investments were replaced in 1967 by the Economic Expansion Act. This Act allowed for the rapid depreciation of assets and allowed for duty free imports of inputs required for exports. Furthermore, taxes on the profits of approved export manufacturers were set at one-tenth of the regular corporate tax rate.[11] As Haggard points out, "given the limited capabilities of local firms, these incentives favored foreign over local investment."[12] In effect, the PAP decided to link the country's economic fortunes to its attractiveness as a destination for international capital.

To enhance its attractiveness to international capital, the government introduced a set of stringent laws aimed at keeping labor costs low. The right of unions to strike was severely curtailed. Working hours were increased and employers were given broad leeway to dismiss workers. Trade union membership fell by one-fifth between 1965 and 1969 alone. As Garry Rodan puts it, "labor was now part of the corporate structure of the Singaporean state."[13]

In addition, Lee opted for a strategy of selective, but substantial, government intervention in the economy. The primary areas of intervention were infrastructural development, institutional support for exporters, and

[8] Haggard 1990, 110.
[9] Haggard 1990, 110.
[10] Rodan 1989, 87.
[11] Haggard 1990, 111.
[12] Haggard 1990, 111.
[13] Rodan 1989, 93.

selected direct government investments.[14] The government established financial institutions like the Development Bank of Singapore to direct low-interest loans to export-oriented industries, the International Trading Company to promote exports, as well as institutions to promote improvements in industrial productivity.[15] An Economic Development Board was also created as a means of coordinating the government's development efforts.[16]

Unlike most developing country contexts where state intervention is high, the government's performance in generating public goods was not sullied by cronyistic relations between business and government. Lee pushed through various measures that served to ensure an arm's length relationship. As Natasha Hamilton-Hart points out, "in the early 1960s the powers of the anti-corruption agency were increased and later changes gave it virtually unfettered powers of investigation and arrest. Prosecuted cases have resulted in significant sentences for those convicted."[17] In addition, Lee substantially raised the salaries of government servants. This served not only as a means of attracting the best talent to government service, but also as a means of reducing the incentives for cultivating close ties with the business community. From all this we can infer that Lee's vision of business–government relations under the labor-intensive exports strategy could not be further from a cronyistic one.

The very success of this strategy in generating high growth and employment meant that it did not last beyond the 1970s. By 1969, it became apparent that Singapore would be facing severe labor shortages in the medium term. In response, the government decided to reduce its reliance on low-wage, labor-intensive production and to place a priority on higher value added products. Gradual steps in this direction culminated in 1978 with the adoption of the so-called Second Industrial Revolution strategy. As Rodan describes it, "extremely generous tax and fiscal incentives were provided for appropriate new [capital intensive] investments, dramatic expansions and improvements were made to social and physical infrastructures, and the government employed direct capital investments with considerable imagination to stimulate and/or initiate favored forms of production."[18] Whereas the priorities of the government shifted from

[14] Rodan 1989, 93.
[15] Rodan 1989, 92–94.
[16] Haggard 1990, 111.
[17] Hamilton-Hart 2002, 81.
[18] Rodan 1989, 142.

low- to high-value added goods, there was no fundamental change in Lee's vision of the government's role as an honest provider of public goods.

Support for the Second Industrial Revolution strategy within the government, however, suffered a severe blow in the face of a severe recession in 1985. The fact that this recession was accompanied by ominous signs of an increase in the popularity of the opposition prompted a serious reassessment of what would be required to establish growth on a more solid footing. Lee commissioned a report entitled, "The Singapore Economy: New Directions," which was spearheaded by his son, Lee Hsien Loong. This report advocated yet another shift of strategy. The central conclusion of the report was that "the driving force of the economy is expected to be the services sector, in particular banking and finance, transport and communications, and international services."[19] The top priority of the government henceforth became one of "heavy investment in social and physical infrastructure to position the city state as a provider of high value added services for the region."[20]

Following this shift in strategy, Singapore once again experienced rapid economic growth, with its GDP increasing by 9.5 percent per annum between 1987 and 1989. The services sector was one of the primary forces behind this increase, with financial and business services alone increasing its share of the GDP from one-fifth of the GDP to one-quarter by the turn of the new decade.[21] By the early 1990s, Singapore had become the fourth largest foreign exchange market in the world after New York, London, and Tokyo.[22]

As W. G. Huff points out, "financial services would not have become an engine of growth in Singapore's economy in the absence of an activist government. One aspect of the government's contribution to the development of financial and business services was the provision of frequently overlooked public goods – the maintenance of honest markets, an environment conducive to easy operation and the stability of the Singapore dollar."[23] Once again it is apparent that, despite an important shift in economic strategy, Lee's aversion to cronyism did not change. In fact, the shift in strategy just mentioned was accompanied by a further enhancement of the

[19] Rodan 1989, 190.
[20] Rodan 1997, 159.
[21] Rodan 1997, 158.
[22] Huff 1994, 341.
[23] Huff 1994, 342.

incentives against cronyistic business–government relations. As Natasha Hamilton-Hart points out, "changes to the corruption law in 1988 further strengthened its punitive scope – to the extent that the bill was criticized for appearing to introduce a presumption of guilt if an accused person dies or absconds during an investigation into corruption."[24]

As far as bank regulation is concerned, in 1971 this issue area was placed under the purview of the newly opened Monetary Authority of Singapore (MAS).[25] The MAS is not considered to be an independent organization because the finance minister generally serves as chairman and takes an active part in all major decisions. Lee entrusted the finance ministership to a succession of his closest confidantes, namely, Hon Sui Sen (1970–83), Tony Tan (1983–85), and Richard Hu (1985–2001).

These appointments amounted to the orthodox solution to the signaling problem. There is indeed no evidence of signaling problems between these bureaucrats, and Lee and his vision of business–government relations indeed prevailed in the realm of bank regulation. The MAS gained a reputation as a stringent regulator over the years, often removing bank directors and imposing large fines for regulatory violations.[26] Foreign and local banks alike were subjected to punishments. Natasha Hamilton-Hart quotes Richard Hu as saying that the government's efforts to stringently enforce prudential regulations were "highly unpopular" with banks in the 1980s.[27] In line with Lee's vision of business government relations, there is no evidence that this led to any softening in the MAS' regulatory approach.

To sum up, although Lee undertook several changes in economic strategy between 1965 and 1990, arm's length business–government relations remained a central part of his vision through all these changes. In line with the expectations of the theory, Lee's authoritarian prime ministership is associated with the appointment of trusted confidantes to signaling positions. There is no evidence of signaling or gridlock problems, and the regulatory outcome was in line with Lee's preferences. In the next section I argue that Lee's departure from the prime ministership in the 1990s did not result in any substantively significant shifts in either the political or in the bank regulatory environment.

---

[24] Hamilton-Hart 2002, 81.
[25] Previously bank regulation fell under the control of the banking commissioner's office.
[26] Hamilton-Hart 2002, 87.
[27] Hamilton-Hart 2002, 98.

6.1.2 *The Political Environment in the 1990s*

In 1990, Lee handed over the prime ministership to his hand-picked successor, Goh Chok Tong. There is little question that Goh, who had served as Lee's deputy, was committed to Lee's policy vision and that this was a necessary condition for his selection in the first place. Lee took the position of senior minister and was the real power behind the prime minister.

Lee took two additional measures to ensure that his departure from the prime ministership did not open the door to policy outcomes that were at variance with his preferences. Lee placed his son, Lee Hsien Loong, in the position of deputy prime minister. In addition, he pushed through a reform of the institution of the presidency. Until Lee relinquished the prime ministership, the presidency was largely a ceremonial position. However, concomitant with Goh's ascent to the prime minister's office, Lee embarked on measures to institute a presidency in which the president would be given substantial powers to veto the prime minister. These measures took the form of an amendment to the constitution, which was approved in January 1991.

As James Cotton describes it, as per this amendment, "the President may now veto the budgets of the government, of key government companies such as Temasek Companies and of statutory boards, including the CPF [the Central Provident Fund] and the Monetary Authority of Singapore. The office-holder may reject appointees to such positions as Chief Justice, Attorney General, Auditor General, membership of the Public Service Commission, and the Chief of the Defense Force. An overseeing role is also accorded to the office regarding the application of the Internal Security Act (which permits detention without trial at the discretion of the executive), the laws relating to the control of religious organizations, and the activities of the Corrupt Practices Investigation Bureau."[28]

In Hussin Mutalib's words, the presidential reform was enacted "to ensure the continuation of the PAP elite's (especially Lee's) model of governance."[29] The goal was to create another office through which Lee could block any prime minister's efforts to diverge from his (Lee's) preferences. Consistent with this goal, the first post-reform president, Ong Teng Cheong, was a trusted long-time associate of Lee's who had previously served as his deputy prime minister. Thus, even after Lee's departure

---

[28] Cotton 1993, 8.
[29] Mutalib 1997, 180. The election rules also made it very difficult for a candidate not supported by the government to run for the presidency.

from the prime ministership, the essentially authoritarian and centralized aspects of Singapore's polity remained solidly in place.

Although there has been some relaxation of the arm's length relationship between business and government in recent years, the change has not fundamentally altered the government's autonomy from business groups. As Linda Lim wrote as late as 1999, "a distinctive feature of Singapore's domestic political economy is the division between the private business elite and the ruling public sector elite.... Although this division has weakened over time – for example, through the increasing popularity of practices such as ... employment by private companies of ruling party members of parliament as paid advisors and the employment of former government officials in highly paid senior management positions in private companies – it remains sufficient to ensure some autonomy in government decision making. Government decision making remains guided primarily by considerations of economic efficiency."[30]

As far as the MAS is concerned, the management of this institution remained largely unchanged for several years after Goh assumed the prime ministership. Lee Kwan Yew's confidante, Richard Hu, who, as mentioned, became finance minister in 1985, remained responsible for the central bank through the 1990s. It is interesting to note that in the four years following the Asian crisis in which Hu was not the chairman of the central bank, this position was occupied by Lee Hsien Loong, Lee Kwan Yew's son. (Subsequently, Lee Hsien Loong became finance minister while retaining the chairmanship of the central bank.) In brief, there is little question that the Ministry of Finance, the Monetary Authority of Singapore, and the prime ministership unambiguously fell under the tight control of officials who shared Lee Kwan Yew's priorities, meaning that the signaling environment for bank regulation remained fundamentally unchanged. Indeed, there is no evidence of signaling problems in this period. As we should expect in an authoritarian environment, there is also no evidence of legislative gridlock. Consistent with the above, I show in the next section that Singapore's bank regulatory environment remained stringent in the 1990s.

6.1.3 Bank Regulation in Singapore in the 1990s

Given that Singapore is a major financial center, it is not surprising that foreign-owned banks predominate the banking sector. One hundred

---

[30] Lim 1999, 112–13.

fifty-three foreign-owned commercial banks and twelve locally owned commercial banks are allowed to operate in Singapore. About 70 percent of the total trade financing comes from the foreign banks.[31] There are four major local banks: the Development Bank of Singapore (DBS); the Overseas Chinese Banking Corporation; the Overseas Union Bank; and the United Overseas Bank. Of the big four, the DBS is controlled by the government. The big four banks control 80 percent of the local bank assets.[32]

There is no evidence that foreign banks were treated any more lightly than local banks when it came to bank regulation. As Natasha Hamilton-Hart discovered from interviews with bankers, the MAS is viewed with fear by foreign and local banks alike.[33] Foreign bankers have even, on occasion, been expelled from Singapore for their failure to observe regulations. As Chow Siow Yue describes the period after Singapore embarked on becoming a financial center, "as liberalization has proceeded, prudential regulations have been strengthened to raise the standards of financial and corporate governance. Banks are efficient and well managed and have some of the highest capital asset ratios in the world. At the micro level, there are efforts to ensure that banks manage their risks prudently. These efforts have contained the incidence of non-performing loans."[34]

In line with this view, Singapore's capital – asset ratio prior to the Asian crisis stood at 20 percent while nonperforming loans stood at 4 percent.[35] The former number was among the highest in the region, while the latter was among the lowest. In addition, reserve requirements were set at 6 percent, and liquid asset requirements were at 18 percent for commercial banks and 10 percent for finance companies, all of which are high by developing-country standards.[36]

To say that Singapore had a stringent bank regulatory environment is not the same as saying that it was perfect. One area of weakness related to exposure to the property sector. The Singapore government controls the land market and also houses 80 percent of the population. Property prices tripled between 1990 and 1996.[37] Linda Lim, a specialist on finance in Singapore, attributes the jump in property prices to the government's

---

[31] US Embassy Singapore 1998, 1.
[32] US Embassy Singapore 1998, 5–6.
[33] Hamilton-Hart 2002, 98.
[34] Yue 1999, 55.
[35] Corsetti et al. 1998.
[36] Yue 1999, 55.
[37] Yue 1999, 59.

policies. As she puts it, "the primary goal of the housing program has always been to win the electoral support of the population by providing decent, affordable housing with a secondary goal of building a sense of community and national commitment through financing occupants' ownership of their public housing units through the forced savings CPF scheme.... Over time policy shifts allowing the resale of Housing Development Board Units and the use of CPF funds to purchase multiple properties and private sector units, together with homeowners' strong inclination to upgrade their properties as affluence spread, resulted in a sharp rise in the prices of both public and private housing units."[38] The exposure of banks to property loans rose to account for 30–40% of all loans.[39]

The government's slow response to the property boom has yet to be attributed to the government's ties to crony businesspeople in the real estate industry, because such ties were hardly significant. In fact, the absence of such ties in all likelihood provided the incentives for the government to eventually respond, in a way that the Malaysian government did not. As Linda Lim has pointed out, the Singaporean government saw its property market policies as being very important for its legitimacy.[40] Arresting the increase in property prices, and thus limiting the capital gains of the country's numerous middle-class property owners, had the potential for damaging this legitimacy. This meant that the government reacted to the property boom a little later than it ideally should have. However, the government did eventually respond. In 1996, the government finally moved to deflate property market values by releasing more public land for housing. This step contributed to the low level of nonperforming loans mentioned previously, although it could have conceivably been even lower if action had been taken a year or two earlier.

The PAP's commitment to stringent regulation was only reinforced by the Asian crisis. The government moved rapidly to enhance its ability to undertake preemptive regulatory actions against potentially weak banks. The Monetary Authority of Singapore announced that it would "monitor and differentiate among institutions by giving the stronger and well managed ones more operational flexibility while maintaining stricter controls on the weaker ones."[41] It also announced that "bank examinations will focus on evaluating risk management processes and internal control

[38] Lim 1999, 111.
[39] Goldstein 1998, 8.
[40] Lim 1999, 110.
[41] MonetaryAuthority of Singapore 1998, 29–30.

systems, instead of detailed transaction testing. This new approach will enable MAS to conduct more focused and frequent examinations."[42] In addition, the MAS tightened information disclosure standards for banks, as a means of increasing market discipline. The ultimate goal of all these changes was to reinforce Singapore's image as a "world class financial center."[43]

To sum up, since independence, the Singaporean chief executive's preference was for arm's length relations between business and government within an authoritarian context. Consistent with the theory of the book, a solution to the signaling problem was always in place, there was no gridlock, and the outcome was a consistently stringent bank regulatory environment.

6.2 HONG KONG

Hong Kong was under British rule in the period that is the focus of this book. The British governor, as the representative of the prime minister of his country, served as the chief executive. I show in this section that, akin to the case in Singapore, a series of chief executives strictly adhered to the principle of arm's length relations between business and government. They also appointed long-trusted bureaucrats who shared this vision to occupy positions at the apex of the financial bureaucracy. In line with the expectations of the theory, there is no evidence of signaling or gridlock problems, and the outcome was consistently in accord with the chief executive's preferences, namely, a stringent bank regulatory environment. Section 6.2.1 describes the vision of governance that was embraced by a succession of British governors. Section 6.2.2 describes the inner circle of banking advisors in the 1990s. Section 6.2.3 describes the bank regulatory environment in the 1990s.

6.2.1 *The Vision of Governance in Hong Kong Under Colonial Rule*

Almost all of Hong Kong's territory was held by the United Kingdom on the basis of a ninety-nine–year lease with China that ran till mid-1997. Under British rule, the territory was run by a governor. Hong Kong's political environment included an executive council (Exco) and a legislative council (Legco). Until 1991, both of these institutions consisted entirely

---

[42] MonetaryAuthority of Singapore 1998, 30.
[43] MonetaryAuthority of Singapore 1998, 31.

of the governor's appointees.[44] Institutional reforms resulted in the emergence of a fully elected Legco by 1995.[45] However, these reforms did not imply the sudden emergence of a democratic state. As Alvin So wrote in 1997, "the existing literature offers a prevailing power dependency perspective of Hong Kong's democracy. In this perspective, the Hong Kong government is seen as a dependent polity, whereby the incumbent London government is responsible for Hong Kong's present, while the Beijing government controls its future. Both Beijing and London command overwhelming resources, especially the coercive ones. Hong Kong people have no credible bargaining strength with either power."[46] In a similar vein, John Flowerdew points out that the "political reform programs only offered what one legislator called 'a drop of democracy.' "[47] In sum, for the entire period that is the concern of this study, Hong Kong remained an authoritarian state.

Given that the political environment was not democratic, the key question then is, what were the preferences of the chief executive? If an economy is largely run on a laissez faire basis, it limits the ability of the government to intervene on behalf of cronies. While Hong Kong was under British rule, a series of governors embraced a laissez faire system, the core of which consisted of a commitment to limit government interference (crony or otherwise) in the economy. As Enright et al. put it, "the clear separation in Hong Kong between the role of the government as referee, and the role of private companies as active players in the economy, is . . . the anomalous product of British colonial arrangements which kept colonial officials aloof from commerce and firmly focused on administration and then on a gentlemanly retirement in England's home counties."[48]

The arrangements that the colonial government established for the conduct of monetary policy were consistent with the priority of limiting interference in the economy. In 1983, the government fixed the exchange rate at 7.8 Hong Kong dollars to the U.S. dollar and delegated monetary policy to an automatic mechanism known as the Currency Board.[49] Under a currency board money supply is automatically determined by foreign reserve levels, and the government cannot intervene to help weak banks with discretionary liquidity injections. It also cannot increase the money supply

---

[44] De Lisle and Lane 1997, 38.
[45] Cheng 1997, 163.
[46] So 1997, 50.
[47] Flowerdew 1998, 1999.
[48] Enright et al. 1997, 30.
[49] A currency board had been in effect since 1935, but had been relinquished in 1972.

to protect banks from high interest rates, as a means of limiting loan defaults. Admittedly, whereas a "pure" currency board arrangement does not allow for the presence of a central banking institution, Hong Kong diverged from the "pure" model by embarking on the establishment of the Hong Kong Monetary Authority (HKMA) in 1988. (The HKMA was finally inaugurated in 1993.) As Barandarian and Shu-ki point out, "since the existence of a currency board implies that money supply is established by demand, the establishment of a parallel central bank in Hong Kong was seen by some as the betrayal of automacity inherent in the currency board system."[50] Top officials in Hong Kong however consistently denied that the presence of the HKMA significantly diluted the automacity with which money supply is determined, pointing out that there was no central bank charter in Hong Kong, and that the goal of the HKMA was merely to smooth short-term currency fluctuations.[51] In support of this view, as long as the HKMA was under British control, there is no evidence that the government did more than intervene at the margins of the currency board mechanism for smoothing purposes. In sum, despite the establishment of the HKMA, the presence of a currency board appears consistent with the colonial rulers' philosophy of limiting government influence over the economy.

Despite all of the above, it must be pointed out that laissez faire, Hong Kong style, did not mean that the government refrained altogether from interventions in the economy. The colonial rulers' conception of laissez faire did allow for state intervention in selected sectors; the government intervened extensively in the realms of education, property, housing, and medical services.[52] However, these interventions were not prompted by cronyistic considerations, but were rather primarily driven by the need to provide essential public goods. One indication of the fact that the colonial power did not have cronyistic priorities comes from the dramatic initiative undertaken by Governor Murray MacLehose to create an anti-corruption agency with real teeth in 1973.[53] As Susan Rose-Ackerman describes it, "officials in the ICAC [the Independent Commission Against Corruption] were paid more than other bureaucrats, and were not subject to transfer to other departments. No one in the ICAC could end up working with a more senior officer who had been subject to prosecution. The ICAC was

---

[50] Barandarian and Shu-ki 1997, 139.
[51] Barandarian and Shu-ki 1997, 140.
[52] Enright et al. 1997, 32.
[53] Flowerdew 1998, 27.

given the power to investigate and prosecute corruption cases, to recommend legal and administrative changes to reduce corrupt incentives, and to engage in a campaign of public education . . . the credibility of the new institution is indicated by the increased number of complaints it received upon establishment and by the high proportion of complaints it received that were not anonymous."[54] Governors following MacLehose continued to support the ICAC, as indicated by the fact there is direct evidence of a decline in perceptions of corruption as well as indirect evidence of a decline in actual corruption in the two decades following the creation of this institution.[55]

The British model of business–government relations was associated with remarkable economic growth. Hong Kong's GDP grew at a rate of approximately 9 percent per annum between 1975 and 1985 and at close to 7 percent thenceforth.[56] These growth rates were achieved while Hong Kong's overwhelmingly became a service-based economy. This change was the direct consequence of economic liberalization in South China in the late 1970s. As manufacturing operations moved across the border to take advantage of cheaper Chinese labor, industry's share of the GDP fell from one-third to one-sixth while the service sector grew from contributing to two-thirds of the GDP to accounting for 83 percent of the GDP by the mid-1990s. Finance, insurance, real estate, and business services alone came to account for 26 percent of the GDP.[57] By the 1990s, Hong Kong had the world's eighth largest and Asia's second largest stock market and the world's fifth largest foreign exchange market.[58] As a major financial center, Hong Kong became home to 500 banks, including offices of 85 of the world's top 100 banks.

As far as bank regulation is concerned, early in the course of the dramatic transition described above, there were three years in which some banks experienced stress. Between 1983 and 1986, seven local banks suffered from large defaults as a consequence of overly aggressive property lending. This served as a spur for tightening regulation. The government took over three of these banks and arranged for the remaining four to be purchased by more robust financial entities. The government also allowed a number of small deposit-taking institutions to fail. In addition,

---

[54] Rose-Ackerman 1999, 160.
[55] Rose-Ackerman 1999, 161.
[56] Enright et al. 1997, 8.
[57] Enright et al. 1997, 14.
[58] Enright et al. 1997, 16.

it introduced a Banking Ordinance in 1986, which explicitly linked bank capital to loan portfolio default risks, introduced more stringent liquidity requirements, and placed limits on lending to shareholders and exposure to any one sector of the economy. The Hong Kong government constantly refined and updated the provisions of the Banking Ordinance in the 1980s, in line with its expressed "policy to keep its supervisory standards in line with international standards."[59]

6.2.2 *The Inner Circle of Banking Advisors in the 1990s*

In 1984, British Prime Minister Margaret Thatcher and the Chinese government agreed on a Joint Declaration specifying the terms and conditions under which the United Kingdom would return Hong Kong to Chinese rule in 1997. As per this declaration, the Chinese agreed to preserve critical features of the system described above for fifty years. Most importantly, the Chinese agreed that "the Hong Kong Special Administrative Region will retain the status of an international financial center and its markets for foreign exchange, gold, securities, and futures will continue. There will be a free flow of capital. The Hong Kong dollar will continue to circulate and be freely convertible."[60]

Subsequently, in 1990, China's Peoples Congress adopted a Basic Law guaranteeing that "the Hong Kong Special Administrative Region shall provide an appropriate economic and legal environment for the maintenance of the status of Hong Kong as an international financial center."[61] As the date for the transition neared, the British began to hand over senior positions in the financial bureaucracy to long-time bureaucrats of local origin.

In the years leading up to the Asian crisis, bank regulation fell under the purview of the Hong Kong Monetary Authority (HKMA). The chief executive of the HKMA from its very inception was Joseph Yam. Yam was a highly respected career bureaucrat who was well known to and trusted by a succession of colonial administrators, working his way up from being a government statistician in 1971, to principal assistant secretary for monetary affairs in 1982, to deputy secretary for monetary affairs in 1985, to director of the office of the exchange fund in 1991.[62]

---

[59] Li 2003, 131–132.
[60] Bowring 1997, 14.
[61] Bowring 1997, 15.
[62] www.info.gov.hk/hkma/ce_comm/chief.html

In his capacity as the chairman of exchange fund advisory committee of the HKMA, the financial secretary of Hong Kong is also involved in the HKMA's management. The position of financial secretary had been held by British officials until 1995, when the position devolved to Donald Tsang. Much like Yam, Tsang was a career bureaucrat who had long been known and trusted by colonial administrators. Tsang, who joined government service in 1967, served as deputy secretary of the special duties branch between 1985 and 1989, in which position he was responsible for the implementation of key provisions of the Joint Declaration. Subsequently, from 1991 to 1993, he served as director general of trade, and from 1993 to 1995 as secretary for the treasury, before assuming the position of financial secretary.[63]

In sum, Yam's and Tsang's preferences were long known to, and well appreciated by, colonial administrators, and their appointments amounted to implementing the orthodox solution to the signaling problem. It is not surprising that there is no evidence of signaling problems between these officials and the governor.

6.2.3 Bank Regulation in Hong Kong in the 1990s

In the 1990s, Hong Kong's bank regulators enforced a capital–asset ratio of 17 percent, which was more than double the level recommended by the Bank for International Settlements.[64] Even the relatively weak banks in Hong Kong were well capitalized.[65] As displayed in Appendix 1, Hong Kong was in close proximity to Singapore in virtually every realm of bank regulation.

This is not to say that the bank regulatory environment was perfect. As mentioned above, the property sector was one of the few areas in which the government intervened directly in the economy. The government controls the market for land in Hong Kong. In a context with extremely low income tax levels, land taxes and sales came to contribute 40 percent of government revenues.[66] This gave the government incentives to push up the price of land by restricting its supply. This, in turn, had the unfortunate side effect of boosting the value of property loans in bank portfolios. As of 1997, 21 percent of total loans were extended to building construction,

---

[63] www.info.gov.hk/info/tsang.htm
[64] Delhaise 1998, 182.
[65] Delhaise 1998, 182.
[66] Lim 1999, 105–6.

property development, and investment, and another 26 percent to individuals for the purchase of residential properties.[67] Many of the loans for residential properties were based on floating interest rates, to a population that was spending 50 percent of its income on mortgage payments.[68] A prolonged period of high interest rates, against which there is little discretionary recourse under a currency board, could clearly put severe pressure on these residential borrowers and potentially provoke massive defaults.[69] In such a context, regulators' decision to demand an exceptionally high capital buffer was indeed appropriate and may be considered as entirely consistent with a preference for having a robust banking sector. (Note that the capital buffer was a massive 50% higher than that observed in Malaysia, despite a similar exposure of banks to the property sector.)

In sum, consistent with what we should expect in an authoritarian environment where the chief executive has arms' length relations with bank owners, the chief executive appointed signalers who shared his vision of business–government relations, and there is no evidence of signaling problems. As per the expectations of the theory, the prudential regulatory environment in the years leading up to the Asian crisis was stringent.

[67] Cheng et al. 1998, 170.
[68] Delhaise 1998, 182–83.
[69] Delhaise 1998, 182–83.

7

Some Concluding Remarks

This concluding chapter is divided into two sections. In the opening section, I summarize my results and address some of the implications and limitations of my analysis. In Section 7.2, I describe my agenda for future research.

7.1 SUMMARY OF RESULTS, IMPLICATIONS, AND LIMITATIONS OF ANALYSIS

In this book, I have attempted to advance the debate over capital flow liberalization in the developing world by studying the determinants of lax bank regulation under liberal capital flows. Aside from cronyism and gridlock, which have previously been identified, I identified a third causal path to lax regulation, namely, the path of incredible signaling. I showed that if a chief executive does not have the freedom to appoint an official who shares his preferences as a signaler of confidential bank regulatory information, the outcome will be an incredible long-term commitment to stringent bank regulation. Using the tools of game theory, I showed that the difference in preferences between a signaler and the chief executive that results in serious miscommunication is very small in the realm of bank regulation. I showed that miscommunication results in an incredible commitment to stringent regulation even in the presence of a chief executive who does not have close ties to bankers, by causing the chief executive to miscalculate his responses to shocks to the banking sector.

I then identified ways to solve signaling problems, such as appointing friends or close associates who share the chief executive's regulatory priorities to senior financial positions. I argued that democracies, unlike authoritarian regimes, are unlikely to be able to credibly commit to always implementing these solutions because chief executives in democracies

130

often face checks to their power over appointments from legislatures. I concluded that when this finding is combined with the greater propensity for legislative gridlock in democracies, which serves as an obstacle to responding to shocks to economy, the implications are clear. Democracies in the developing world are exceptionally ill suited to operating under liberal capital flows from the perspective of bank regulation.

The theoretical apparatus that justifies the above claims is based on the theory of "cheap talk" games. Aside from presenting cheap talk models to justify my claims about miscommunication, I offered case studies of all the Asian countries that had undergone capital account liberalization in the early 1990s. I showed that all the democracies in the sample experienced unresolved signaling problems at some point. The consequence was lax regulation even when the chief executive was not a crony capitalist and had substantial regulatory decision-making powers. In contrast, I showed that all the authoritarian countries in the sample found solutions to the signaling problem. Regulatory outcomes in authoritarian environments were thus in line with whether the chief executive had crony links with bank owners. In the presence of such links, the outcome was lax regulation. In the absence of such links, the outcome was stringent regulation.

The obvious question that is raised by my analysis is, why have many *developed* democracies been able to operate under liberal capital flows without falling prey to major signaling problems or lax regulation? While a definitive answer to this question must await a more systematic analysis, there is one plausible explanation, namely, regulatory bureaucrats' autonomy from politicians. In the developed world, bank regulation is frequently placed under the control of either an independent central bank or a free-standing regulatory organization that is legally insulated from politicians, led by a powerful technocratic official who has arm's length relations with bank owners. Since the technocrat a) will at least have a preference for a moderately robust banking sector, and b) has the skills to study banks' accounting statements himself, as well as c) has the power to make regulatory decisions unencumbered by politicians, the outcome will be stringent regulation. In effect, with an independent and technocratic regulatory bureaucracy we can get a result that is identical to what we observe in developing-country environments with very few checks where the chief executive has arm's length relations with bank owners, even in the context of a democracy.

The problem in the developing world is that it has proved remarkably difficult to establish technocratically led institutions for financial governance that are genuinely independent of politicians. Legal provisions that are purported to guarantee bureaucratic independence are often not honored. For instance, as Cukierman, Webb, and Neyapti have found in a widely cited study, in sharp contrast to the observed facts in the developed world, legal central bank independence is not associated with a superior record in controlling inflation in the developing world.[1] In addition, Sylvia Maxfield has found that central bank "independence" varies in accord with the preferences of politicians in developing countries.[2] In the realm of bank regulation, there are hardly any institutions in the developing world that can plausibly claim to be genuinely independent of the political leadership.

The only case in the developing world where a claim of modest independence can even be reasonably attempted is for the Chilean central bank. As Delia Boylan has shown, the outgoing authoritarian regime, led by Augusto Pinochet, made it a precondition for democratization that the autonomy of the central bank be protected by numerous legal provisions.[3] Furthermore, the pre-conditions for democratization included an exceptionally prominent role for the military in the post-transition environment, which helped it to serve as a guarantor for these provisions. As Appendix 1 shows, Chile did indeed succeed in having a stringent regulatory environment. This suggests that the discouraging prospects for credible long-term commitments to stringent regulation in developing democracies, as stated, may be contingent on the absence of independent regulatory bureaucracies. Before one becomes too hopeful about the prospects for stringent regulation in developing democracies, however, it is important to keep in mind that Chile's transition to democracy was highly idiosyncratic, if not unique. It is highly questionable if the Chilean experience of transition is replicable, or even normatively desirable. Furthermore, Chile did not truly test its regulators to the challenges of operating under liberal capital flows in the 1990s, because it maintained substantial controls on short-term flows.[4] Thus, it remains an open question as to whether Chile's commitment to stringent regulation would have held up in the face of truly liberal capital flows.

I conclude this section with some possible objections to the mode of analysis that I have adopted for this project. First, I have given little

---

[1] Cukierman, Webb, and Neyapti 1992.
[2] Maxfield 1997.
[3] Boylan 2001.
[4] As I show in Appendix 1, Chile had high levels of capital controls.

consideration to the possibility that bank regulation is an inexact science, and that lax regulation, far from being intended, resulted from this very inexactness. In other words, the lax regulators may have generated less than stringent environments against their intentions because of the lack of clarity about what constitutes a stringent regulatory environment. This is certainly possible in theory, but I am uncertain why weak regulators could not have used Singapore or Hong Kong as a model for a stringent bank regulatory environment. Furthermore, even if one plausibly grants a role to the inexactness of bank regulation as a science, the very distance between the stringency of the regulatory environments established by Singapore and Hong Kong and those established by the lax regulators, displayed in Figure 1.1 in Chapter 1, suggests a margin of error that goes well beyond what could occur from a misunderstanding of what constitutes stringent regulation.

Second, some may object to the fact that actors' utility in my analysis derives from entirely self-serving motives. This may strike some as an exceedingly pessimistic assumption. Politicians may be influenced by other considerations, such as ideas. While this is entirely possible in theory, I, like other contributors to the literature, have been unable to find a way to systematically relate variations in receptivity to ideas to the actual regulatory outcomes in the field. This is not to say that ideas do not matter, but rather that it is exceedingly difficult to identify which actors were more or less receptive to which ideas in the Asian context.

Third, for the formal signaling model, I have exclusively considered one aspect of bank regulation, namely, the level of shareholder capital relative to expected defaults. This may strike some as unusually restrictive given that an assessment of the overall stringency of the bank regulatory environment includes the other considerations listed in Appendix 1. However, this choice is driven by the consideration that signaling problems are only worthy of attention in realms of incomplete and asymmetric information. I chose to focus on capitalization in the formal signaling model for the simple reason that the assessment of expected defaults, and the appropriate capital response, is the one area of regulation where conditions of incomplete and asymmetric information are extremely likely to prevail.

Finally, my entire analysis is based on the assumption that actors are rational, that is, that they choose strategies that maximize their utility. This may strike some as an overly restrictive assumption. Certainly it would be possible to produce a richer analysis that allows for the irrationality of actors. However, authors are constrained in their choice of analytical techniques by the skills they command. In my case, I admit that my analytical skills are limited to rigorously evaluating the actions of rational actors.

7.2 AN AGENDA FOR FUTURE RESEARCH

The framework of analysis that I have presented in this book is by no means applicable only to the realm of bank regulation. It potentially can be applied to any issue area in which policy outcomes hinge on the communication of information from a relatively well-informed to a less-informed decision maker. For instance, is the incidence of slow responses to emerging fiscal disasters correlated with the presence of environments where it is difficult to credibly signal adverse trends to politicians? Do countries move exceptionally slowly to acquire lines of credit from the IMF when a decline in a country's debt-servicing capabilities cannot be credibly signaled to the chief executive? Both of these questions are currently on my research agenda.

In this book, I focused exclusively on an in-depth analysis of signaling problems in a few cases. I was constrained from conducting a statistical test by the paucity of developing countries operating under liberal capital flows. As more developing countries liberalize, a statistical test becomes more feasible, and this is certainly on my research agenda.

Finding answers to the questions listed above only constitutes a small part of my research agenda. If there is any area in political science that has been neglected by formal modelers, it is political institutions in developing countries. There is no obvious reason why this should be the case. My research agenda thus includes a close examination of numerous developing-country institutions through the lens of formal game theory. This research agenda includes, but also goes beyond, the analysis of constitutionally established institutions such as legislatures, which are common objects of study in the developed world. In developing-country contexts, many important decisions are made behind closed doors in issue-specific institutions, such as the inner circle examined in this book. Given the prevalence of such institutions, the systematic study of more issue-specific institutions has the potential for enhancing our understanding of important policy choices in the developing world. My research agenda thus includes the formal analysis of such institutions in the realms of trade and fiscal policy. I hope that my research program will provide a stimulus for more formal modelers to engage in the study of developing-country institutions.

Appendix I

The World Bank's Evaluation of Bank Regulatory Environments

In 1997, prior to the implementation of post-crisis reforms, the World Bank evaluated the bank regulatory environments of twelve countries on six criteria known as CAMELOT: capitalization, loan classification, management, liquidity, operating environment, and transparency. The countries were rank ordered in each of these areas, and their rank scores were added up to yield an overall score. Countries were then assigned to five different categories of stringency based on the clustering of points, with the top two categories being indicative of stringent regulation. Of the twelve countries, seven were the Asian countries with liberal capital flows that are considered in this book, while the remaining five were Latin American countries. Table A.1 shows how these countries ranked on each of the components of regulation. Note that of the two democracies that had stringent bank regulatory environments, the commitment of one (Argentina) collapsed in the late 1990s. As for the second, Chile, the country's regulatory record was achieved under a regime with substantial capital controls, meaning that we have no way of knowing if it would have been robust to massive unrestricted capital inflows. (Chile's score on the IMF's capital controls index was 0.89 out of a possible 1 in 1996, with 1 indicating a closed environment.[1] By way of comparison, the most closed economy of the ones studied in this book was South Korea, with a score of 0.7.)

A detailed description of each of the regulatory measures is available in Caprio (1998).

---

[1] Johnston et al. 1999, 90.

Appendix Table A.1 *Rank Order on Individual Areas of Regulation*

Country	Stringency Category	Total Score	Capital	Loan Classification (Identification of Nonperforming Loans)	Management	Liquidity	Operating Environment (Property Rights + Creditor Rights + Enforcement of the Legal System)	Transparency
Singapore	1	16	1	6	2	5	1	1
Argentina	1 (Collapsed after 1997)	21(Collapsed after 1997)	1	4	3	4	7	2
Hong Kong	2	21	3	9	1	2	2	4
Chile (had capital controls)	2	25	5	1	4	8	5	2
Brazil (had capital controls)	3	30	7	3	4	3	8	5
Peru (had capital controls)	3	35	5	2	6	1	11	10
Malaysia	4	41	5	9	8	8	3	8
Colombia	4	44	3	4	11	6	10	10
South Korea	4	45	7	9	10	11	3	5
Philippines	4	47	4	6	7	7	11	12
Thailand	5	52	7	12	12	8	6	7
Indonesia	5	52	7	8	9	12	8	8

Source: Caprio 1998.

Appendix II

Verbal Description of the Equilibrium with Two Signalers

Assume, strictly for the time being, that the chief executive has a posterior belief that the signaled value of z is true only when the messages sent by both signalers agree. Assume, also strictly for the time being, that when the messages disagree he believes that z lies between $\varpi - 2x_{s1}$ and $\varpi + 2x_{s1}$. (At the end of this section, I demonstrate that these beliefs are consistent with the senders' strategies.)

Given the above posterior beliefs, the chief executive will find it optimal to choose $k = z$ when the messages agree. This is the case because, given that $x = k - z$, $k = z$ will yield $x = 0$, which is his ideal point. Both senders will prefer to signal the true value of z, if the chief executive's choice when the messages do not agree will yield a value of x further from both their ideal points than x_c. Because ω is uniformly distributed, and given that when the messages disagree the chief executive believes that it lies between $\varpi - 2x_{s1}$ and $\varpi + 2x_{s1}$, the chief executive's choice of k when the messages disagree is ϖ. (This choice maximizes his expected utility when z lies between these values, because it minimizes the expected distance of x from his ideal point.) Given that $x = k - z$, the chief executive's choice of $k = \varpi$ when the messages disagree yields outcomes that are to the left of $-2x_{s1}$ when $z > \varpi + 2x_{s1}$ and to the right of 2_{xs1} when $z < \varpi - 2x_{s1}$. Thus, when z takes these values, both senders would find it optimal to send the same true message because x_c, which as described above is the outcome when they do so, offers greater utility to both senders than these extreme outcomes.

However, when z lies between ϖ and $\varpi + 2x_{s1}$, the chief executive's choice of $k = \varpi$ when the messages disagree yields outcomes that are between $-2x_{s1}$ and x_c. When z lies between these values, it is Sender 2's best response to signal a different value of z from Sender 1 because the outcome yielded from conflicting signals is closer to his ideal point than x_c,

137

which would be the outcome if both senders sent matching true signals. Analogously, when z lies between $\varpi - 2x_{s1}$ and ϖ, the chief executive's choice of $k = \varpi$ when the messages disagree yields outcomes that are between x_c and $2x_{s1}$. The outcomes that would result from conflicting signals are preferable to Sender 1 because they are closer to his ideal point than x_c, which would be the outcome if both senders sent matching true messages. Given that communication of the true value of z is not optimal for one of the senders when it takes values between $\varpi - 2x_{s1}$ and $\varpi + 2x_{s1}$, rendering credible communication of the true value by the other sender impossible, the two senders lose nothing from randomly selecting values of z between the above values as signals, when z falls between the above values. (The policy outcome will be the same as that which would result from only one sender signaling the true value, because the signals will continue to conflict. The signals will continue to conflict because, given that we are considering a continuous space, there is zero probability that a randomized signal will take any particular value.)

Given that the senders send matching true signals only when z takes values greater than $\varpi + 2x_{s1}$ and less than $\varpi - 2x_{s1}$ and send conflicting, inaccurate signals when z takes values between $\varpi - 2x_{s1}$ and $\varpi + 2x_{s1}$, the chief executive's posterior belief that the signaled value of z is true only when the signals sent by both senders agree, and that z lies between $\varpi - 2x_{s1}$ and $\varpi + 2x_{s1}$ when the signals disagree, is consistent with the senders' strategies.

Thus, there is a Perfect Bayesian Equilibrium that has the characteristics described in the proposition.

Appendix III

Formal Proof of Equilibrium with Two Signalers

III.1 FORMAL DEFINITION OF SOLUTION CONCEPT

A Perfect Bayesian Equilibrium is a set of strategies, $k^*(m_1, m_2)$, $m_1^*(z, m_2, k)$, and $m_2^*(z, m_1, k)$, and posterior beliefs, $g^*(z; m_1, m_2)$, such that:

1. $m_1(z, m_2, k) \in \arg\max EU_{s1}$, given $k^*(m_1, m_2)$ and $m_2^*(z, m_1, k)$.
2. $m_2(z, m_1, k) \in \arg\max EU_{s2}$, given $k^*(m_1, m_2)$ and $m_1^*(z, m_2, k)$.
3. $k^*(m_1, m_2) \in \arg\max_k \int_0^{0.15} u_c(k; z) g^*(z, m_1, m_2) dz$.
4. $g^*(z; m_1, m_2) = \Pr(\omega = z | m_1^*, m_2^*)$ as per Bayes' rule.

Proposition: There exists a Perfect Bayesian Equilibrium in which:

1. $m_1^*(z, m_2, k) = z$ if $z < \varpi - 2x_{s1}$ or $z > \varpi + 2x_{s1}$, and s_1 randomizes with equal probability over $[\varpi - 2x_{s1}, \varpi + 2x_{s1}]$ otherwise.
2. $m_2^*(z, m_1, k) = z$ if $z < \varpi - 2x_{s1}$ or $z > \varpi + 2x_{s1}$, and s_2 randomizes with equal probability over $[\varpi - 2x_{s1}, \varpi + 2x_{s1}]$ otherwise.
3. $k^*(m_1, m_2) = z$ if $m_1 = m_2$, and ϖ otherwise.
4. If $m_1 = m_2$, $g^*(z; m_1, m_2) = 1$. If $m_1 \neq m_2$, $g^*(z; m_1, m_2) = 0$ for all $z \notin [\varpi - 2x_{s1}, \varpi + 2x_{s1}]$.

Proof. The proof is in four parts.

1. Show that $m_1(z, m_2, k) \in \arg\max EU_{s1}$, given $k^*(m_1, m_2)$, and $m_2^*(z, m_1, k)$. I address each component of $m_1^*(z, m_2, k)$ in turn.
   a. $m_1^*(z, m_2, k) = z$ if $z < \varpi - 2x_{s1}$. The policy outcome, x, resulting from $m_1 \neq m_2$ is as follows. From the proposed equilibrium, note

139

that when $m_1 \neq m_2$, $k^*(m_1, m_2) = \varpi$. When $z < \varpi - 2x_{s1}$ and c chooses ϖ, $x > 2x_{s1}$. When $m_1 = m_2 = z$, $k^*(m_1, m_2) = z$, yielding $x = 0$, which yields s_1 greater utility than $x > 2x_{s1}$.

b. $m_1^*(z, m_2, k) = z$ if $z > \varpi + 2x_{s1}$. If $m_1 \neq m_2$, c chooses ϖ, yielding $x < -2x_{s1}$. This outcome offers less utility to s_1 than $x = 0$, which would be the outcome if $m_1 = m_2 = z$.

c. s_1 randomizes with equal probability over $[\varpi - 2x_{s1}, \varpi + 2x_{s1}]$ if $z \in [\varpi - 2x_{s1}, \varpi + 2x_{s1}]$. When $z \in [\varpi - 2x_{s1}, \varpi + 2x_{s1}]$, s_2 is randomizing between these values. Thus, s_1 cannot confirm s_2's signal, and his choice of signal has no effect on the chief executive's decision. (The chief executive will believe that $z \in [\varpi - 2x_{s1}, \varpi + 2x_{s1}]$ irrespective of what s_1 does.)

2. Show that $m_2(z, m_1, k) \in \arg\max EU_{s2}$, given $k^*(m_1, m_2)$ and $m_1^*(z, m_2, k)$. Use the same logic as above and reverse the labels of the signalers.

3. Show that $k^*(m_1, m_2) \in \arg\max_k \int_0^{0.15} u_c(k; z) g^*(z, m_1, m_2) dz$.

a. If $g^*(z; m_1, m_2) = 1$, which is the case when $m_1 = m_2$, $k = z$ is optimal for the chief executive because it yields his ideal point, $x = 0$.

b. If $g^*(z; m_1, m_2) = 0$ for all $z \notin [\varpi - 2x_{s1}, \varpi + 2x_{s1}]$, which is the case when $m_1 \neq m_2$, c chooses k to maximize:

$$\int_{\varpi - 2xs1}^{\varpi + 2xs1} -(k - z)^2 g^*(z, m_1, m_2) dz.$$

This yields $k^*(m_1, m_2) = \varpi$.

4. Establish the consistency of $g^*(z; m_1, m_2)$. This was already established in Part 1(c).

III.2   COROLLARY

The above equilibrium becomes fully babbling if $x_{s1} \geq 0.0375$.

If $x_{s1} \geq .0375$, $\varpi + 2x_{s1} \geq 0.15$ and $\varpi - 2x_{s1} \leq 0$.

Bibliography

Abdollahian, M.A., J. Kugler, and H.L. Root. 2000. Economic Crisis and the Future of Oligarchy. In *Institutional Reform and Democratic Consolidation in Korea*, L. Diamond and D.C. Shin, Eds. Stanford, CA: Hoover Institution Press.

Abueva, J. 1997. Philippine Democratization and the Consolidation of Democracy Since the 1986 Revolution: An Overview of the Main Issues, Trends, and Prospects. In *Democratization: Philippine Perspectives*, F. Miranda, Ed. Dilimoan, Quezon City: University of the Philippines Press.

Ammar, S. 1997. Can a Developing Country Manage its Macro Economy? The Case of Thailand. In *Thailand's Boom and Bust*, A. Siamwalla, Ed. Bangkok: Thai Development Research Institute.

Ammar, S. and S. Orapin. 1998. *Responding to the Thai Crisis*. Bangkok: United Nations Development Program.

Amsden, A. 1994. The World Bank's East Asian Miracle: Economic Growth and Public Policy. *World Development* 22:4, 615–670.

Anusorn, L. 2000. Thailand. In *Political Party Systems and Democratic Development in East and Southeast Asia: Volume I*, W. Sachsenröder and U.E. Frings. Aldershot, Hampshire, UK: Ashgate.

Ariff, M., M. Chang, A. Kadir, O. Ean, and E. Lae-Imm. 1998. *Currency Turmoil, and the Malaysian Economy: Genesis, Prognosis, and Response*. Kuala Lumpur: Malaysian Institute of Economic Research.

Arndt, H.W. 1997. The Rupiah Crisis: An Alternative View. *Bulletin of Indonesian Economic Studies* 33(3):53–56.

Asia Money Magazine. (www.asiamoney.com)

Asian Development Bank. 1999. *Asian Development Outlook 1999*. New York: Oxford University Press.

Athukorala, P.-C. 1998. Malaysia. In *East Asia in Crisis: From Being a Miracle to Needing One?*, R.H. McLeod and R. Garnaut, Eds. London: Routledge.

Austen-Smith, D. 1990. Information Transmission in Debate. *American Journal of Political Science* 34:124–52.

Austen-Smith, D. and W.H. Riker. 1987. Asymmetric Information and the Coherence of Legislation. *American Political Science Review* 81:897–918.

Backman, M. 1999. *Asian Eclipse: Exposing the Dark Side of Business in Asia.* Singapore: John Wiley & Sons.

Bangko Sentral ng Pilipinas. 1993. *Republic Act No. 7653: The New Central Bank Act.* Manila: Bangko Sentral ng Pilipinas.

———. 1997. *Fifth Annual Report.* Manila: Bangko Sentral ng Pilipinas.

———. 1998a. *Sixth Annual Report.* Manila: Bangko Sentral ng Pilipinas.

———. 1998b. *The Philippines: Onward to Recovery.* Manila: Bangko Sentral ng Pilipinas.

———. 1998c. *Key Economic Issues.* Manila: Bangko Sentral ng Pilipinas.

———. 1999a. *BSP Measures Implemented to Address the Currency Crisis.* Manila: Bangko Sentnal ng Pilipinas.

———. 1999b. *Financial Sector Reforms in the Philippines 1981–1998.* Manila: Bangko Sentral ng Pilipinas.

———. 1999c. *The Philippines: Sustaining the Recovery.* Manila: Bangko Sentnal ng Pilipinas.

Bank of Indonesia. 1996. *Report for the Financial Year 1995/96.* Jakarta: Bank Indonesia.

———. 1997. *Report for the Financial Year 1996/97.* Jakarta: Bank Indonesia.

———. 1998. *1997–1998 Annual Report.* Jakarta: Bank of Indonesia.

Bank Negara Malaysia. 1996. *Annual Report 1996.* Kuala Lumpur: Bank Negara Malaysia.

———. 1997a. *Annual Report 1997.* Kuala Lumpur: Bank Negara Malaysia.

———. 1997b. *Quarterly Bulletin: Third Quarter 1997.* Kuala Lumpur: Bank Negara Malaysia.

———. 1998a. *Annual Report 1998.* Kuala Lumpur: Bank Negara Malaysia.

———. 1998b. *Quarterly Bulletin: First Quarter 1998.* Kuala Lumpur: Bank Negara Malaysia.

———. 1999. *Annual Report 1999.* Kuala Lumpur: Bank Negara Malaysia.

Bank of Thailand. 1992. *50 Years of the Bank of Thailand.* Bangkok: Bank of Thailand.

———. 1997. *Annual Report 1997.* Bangkok: Bank of Thailand.

———. 1998a. Focus on the Thai Crisis. *Bank of Thailand Economic Focus* 2, no. 2. Economic Research Department. Bangkok: Bank of Thailand.

———. 1998b. Asset Price Inflation: Developments and Policy Issues. *Bank of Thailand Economic Focus* 2, no. 1. Economic Research Department. Bangkok: Bank of Thailand.

Banyong, P. and S. Supavud. 1997. How to Avoid the Fall of Thailand. Manuscript.

Barandarian, E. and T. Shu-ki. 1997. One Country, Two Currencies: Monetary Relations Between Hong Kong and China. In *Hong Kong Under Chinese Rule: The Economic and Political Implications of Reversion*, W.I. Cohen and L. Zhao, Eds. New York: Cambridge University Press.

Beck, T., G. Clark, A. Groff, P. Keefer, and P. Walsh. 2001. *New Tools in Comparative Political Economy: The Data Base of Political Institutions.* (www.worldbank.org).

Beng-Huat, C. 2001. Arrested Development: Democratization in Singapore. In *Singapore*, G. Rodan, Ed. Sydney: Ashgate.

Bibliography

Berg, A. 1999. The Asian Crisis: Causes, Policy Responses, and Outcomes. IMF Working Paper. (http://imf.org/external/pubs/ft/wp/1999/wp99138.pdf).

Bhagwati, J. 1998. The Capital Myth. *Foreign Affairs* 77(3):7–12.

Bongini, P., S. Claeesens, and G. Ferri. 2001. The Political Economy of Distress in East Asian Financial Institutions. *Journal of Financial Services Research* 19(1):5–25.

Boylan, D. 2001. *Defusing Democracy: Central Bank Autonomy and the Transition from Authoritarian Rule*. Ann Arbor: University of Michigan Press.

Bresnan, J. 1993. *Managing Indonesia: The Modern Political Economy*. New York: Columbia University Press.

Bowring, P. 1997. Hong Kong as an International Commercial Center. In *Hong Kong Under Chinese Rule: The Economic and Political Implications of Reversion*, W.I. Cohen and L. Zhao, Eds. New York: Cambridge University Press.

Buckley, R. 1997. *Hong Kong: The Road to 1997*. New York: Cambridge University Press.

Bunbongkarn, S. 1996. Elections and Democratization in Thailand. In *The Politics of Elections in Southeast Asia*, R.H. Taylor, Ed. Cambridge: Cambridge University Press.

Burns, J.P. 1997. Civil Service Systems in Transition: Hong Kong, China, and 1997. In *The Challenge of Hong Kong's Reintegration with China*, M.K. Chan, Ed. Hong Kong: Hong Kong University Press.

Caprio, G. 1998. *Banking on Crises: Expensive Lessons from Recent Financial Crises*. Washington D.C.: World Bank (http://econ.worldbank.org/docs/686.pdf)

Caprio, G. and P. Honohan. 1999. Restoring Banking Stability: Beyond Supervised Capital Requirements. *Journal of Economic Perspectives* 13(4):43–64.

Caprio, G. Jr. and D. Klingebiel. 1997. Bank Insolvency: Bad Luck, Bad Policy, or Bad Banking? *Annual World Bank Conference on Development Economics 1996*. Washington D.C.: The World Bank.

Chai-anan, S. 1997. Old Soldiers Never Die, They Are Just Bypassed: The Military, Bureaucracy, and Globalization. In *Political Change in Thailand: Democracy and Participation*, K. Hewison, Ed. London: Routledge.

Chang, H.-J. 1998. Korea: The Misunderstood Crisis. *World Development* 26(8): 1555–61.

Cheng, J.Y.S. Political Participation in Hong Kong: Trends in the 1990s. In *Hong Kong Under Chinese Rule: The Economic and Political Implications of Reversion*, W.I. Cohen and L. Zhao, Eds. New York: Cambridge University Press.

Cheng, Y.-S., W. Marn-Heong, and C. Findlay. 1998. Singapore and Hong Kong. In *East Asia in Crisis: From Being a Miracle to Needing One?* R.H. McLeod and R. Garnaut, Eds. New York: Routledge.

Cheung, A.B.L. 2002. Transformation of Hong Kong's Civil Service System. In *Crisis and Transformation in China's Hong Kong*, M.K. Chan and A.Y. So. Armonk, NY: M.E. Sharpe.

Choi, J.-W. 2002. Regulatory Forbearance and Financial Crisis in South Korea. *Asian Survey*, 42(2):251–275.

Christiansen, S., A. Siamwalla, and P. Vichayanond. 1997. Institutional and Political Bases of Growth Inducing Politics. In *Thailand's Boom and Bust*, A. Siamwalla, Ed. Bangkok: Thai Development Research Institute.

Chung-si, A. and H. Jaung. 1999. South Korea. In *Democratic Governance and Economic Performance: East and South East Asia*, I. Marsh, J. Blondel, and T. Inoguchi, Eds. Tokyo: U.N. Press.

Clifford, M. 1998. *Troubled Tiger: Businessmen, Bureaucrats, and Generals in South Korea*. Armonk, NY: M.E. Sharpe.

Cole, D.C. and B.F. Slade. 1996. *Building a Modern Financial System*. Cambridge: Cambridge University Press.

———. 1998. Why Has Indonesia's Financial Crisis Been So Bad? *Bulletin of Indonesian Economic Studies* 34(2):61–66.

Corsetti, G., P. Pesenti, and N. Roubini. 1998. What Caused the Asian Currency and Financial Crisis? Part I: A Macroeconomic Overview (http://pages.stern.nyu.edu/~nroubini/asia/).

Cotton, J. 1993. Political Innovation in Singapore: The Presidency, the Leadership, and the Party. In *Singapore Changes Guard*, G. Rodan, Ed. Melbourne: Longman.

Cox, G. 1997. *Making Votes Count: Strategic Coordination in the World's Electoral Systems*. Cambridge: Cambridge University Press.

Crawford, V. and J. Sobel. 1982. Strategic Information Transmission. *Econometrica* 50:1431–51.

Crouch, H. 1996. *Government and Society in Malaysia*. Singapore: Allen & Unwin.

Cukierman, A., S. Webb, and B. Neyapti. 1992. Measuring Central Bank Independence and its Effects on Economic Outcomes. *The World Bank Economic Review* 6(3):353–98.

de Dios, E.S. 1997. Economic Outcomes and Philippine Democratization. In *Democratization: Philippine Perspectives*, F. Miranda, Ed. Dilimoan, Quezon City: University of the Philippines Press.

———. 1998. Philippine Economic Growth: Can it Last? In *The Philippines: New Directions in Domestic Policy and Foreign Relations*, D. Timberman, Ed. Singapore: Asia Society.

Delhaise, P.F. 1998. *Asia in Crisis: The Implosion of the Banking and Finance Systems*. Singapore: John Wiley & Sons.

De Lisle, J. and K.P. Lane. 1997. Cooking the Rice Without Cooking the Goose: The Rule of Law, the Battle Over Business, and the Quest for Prosperity in Hong Kong after 1997. In *Hong Kong Under Chinese Rule: The Economic and Political Implications of Reversion*, W.I. Cohen and L. Zhao, Eds. New York: Cambridge University Press.

Demirguc-Kunt, A. and E. Detragiache. 1997. The Determinants of Banking Crises (http://econ.worldbank.org/docs/472.pdf).

Dewatripont, M. and J. Tirole. 1994. *The Prudential Regulation of Banks*. Cambridge, MA: MIT Press.

Dimbleby, J. 1998. *The Last Governor: Chris Patten and the Handover of Hong Kong*. New York: Warner, Little Brown.

Doner, R. and D. Unger. 1993. The Politics of Finance in Thai Economic Development. In *The Politics of Finance in Developing Countries*, S. Haggard, C. Lee, and S. Maxfield, Eds. Ithaca, NY: Cornell University Press.

Eichengreen, B. 1998. *Capital Controls: Capital Idea or Capital Folly?* (http://emlab.berkeley.edu/users/eichengr/capcontrols.pdf).

———. 1999. *Toward a New International Financial Architecture*. Washington, D.C.: Institute for International Economics.

Enright, M.J., E.E. Scott, and D. Dodwell. 1997. *The Hong Kong Advantage*. New York: Oxford University Press.

Evans, P. 1995. *Embedded Autonomy: States and Industrial Transformation*. Princeton, NJ: Princeton University Press.

Fischer, S. 1999. On the Need for an International Lender of Last Resort. *Journal of Economic Perspectives* 13(4):85–104.

Flowerdew, J. 1998. *The Final Years of British Hong Kong*. New York: Macmillan.

Folkerts-Landau, D. and C.J. Lindgren. 1998. *Toward a Framework for Financial Stability*. Washington, D.C.: International Monetary Fund.

Frieden, J. 1994. Invested Interests: The Politics of National Economic Policies in a World of Global Finance. *International Organization* 45(4).

Furman, J. and J.E. Stiglitz. 1998. Economic Crises: Evidence and Insights from East Asia. Paper prepared for the Brookings Panel on Economic Activity, Sept. 3–4.

Gibbons, R. 1992. *Game Theory for Applied Economists*. Princeton, NJ: Princeton University Press.

Gilligan, T.W. and K. Krehbiel. 1987. Collective Decision Making and Standing Committees: An Informational Rationale for Restrictive Amendment Procedures. *Journal of Law, Economics and Organization* 3:287–335.

———. 1989. Asymmetric Information and Legislative Rules with a Heterogenous Committee. *American Journal of Political Science* 33:459–90.

Gochoco-Bautista, M.S. 2000. *The Past Performance of the Philippine Banking Sector and Challenges in the Postcrisis Period*. Manila: Asian Development Bank.

Goldstein, M. 1997. *The Case for an International Banking Standard*. Washington, D.C.: Institute for International Economics.

———. 1998. *The Asian Financial Crisis: Causes, Cures, and Systemic Implications*. Washington, D.C.: Institute for International Economics.

Gomez, E.T. 1991. *Money Politics In the Barisan Nasional*. Selangor, Malaysia: Forum Publications.

———. 1994. *Political Business: Corporate Involvement of Malaysian Political Parties*. Townsville, Australia: Centre for South-East Asian Studies.

———. 1999. Malaysia. In *Democracy, Governance and Economic Performance: East and Southeast Asia*, I. March, J. Blondel, and T. Inoguchi, Eds. Tokyo: United Nations University Press.

———. 2000. Malaysia. In *Political Party Systems and Democratic Governance in East and South East Asia*, W. Sachsenroeder and U. Frings, Eds. Brookfield, VT: Ashgate.

———. and K.S. Jomo. 1997. *Malaysia's Political Economy*. Cambridge: Cambridge University Press.

Government of Malaysia. 1999. *Status of the Malaysian Economy*. Kuala Lumpur: Government of Malaysia.

Haggard, S. 1990. The Political Economy of the Philippine Debt Crisis. In *Economic Crisis and Policy Choice: The Politics of Adjustment in the Third World*, J.M. Nelson, Ed. Princeton, NJ: Princeton University Press.

———. 2000. *The Political Economy of the Asian Financial Crisis*. Washington, D.C.: Institute for International Economics.

Haggard, S. and R.R. Kaufman. 1992. Institutions and Economic Adjustment. In *The Politics of Economic Adjustment*, S. Haggard and R.R. Kaufman, Eds. Princeton, NJ: Princeton University Press.

———. 1995. *The Political Economy of Democratic Transitions*. Princeton, NJ: Princeton University Press.

Haggard, S. and A. MacIntyre. 2000. The Political Economy of the Asian Financial Crisis: Korea and Thailand Compared. In *The Asian Financial Crisis and the Architecture of Global Finance*, G.W. Noble and J. Ravenhill, Eds. New York: Cambridge University Press, pp. 1–35.

Hahm, J.-H. and F.S. Mishkin. 2000. Causes of the Korean Financial Crisis: Lessons for Policy. Manuscript.

Hamilton-Hart, N. 2000. Indonesia: Reforming the Institutions of Financial Governance. In *The Asian Financial Crisis and the Architecture of Global Finance*, G. Noble and J. Ravenhill, Eds. New York: Cambridge University Press.

———. 2002. *Asian States, Asian Bankers: Central Banking in South East Asia*. Ithaca, NY: Cornell University Press.

Handley, P. 1997. More of the Same? Politics and Business, 1987–1996. In *Political Change in Thailand: Democracy and Participation*, K. Hewison, Ed. London: Routledge.

Heller, W.B., P. Keefer, and M.D. McCubbins. 1998. Political Structure and Economic Liberalization: Conditions and Cases from the Developing World. In *The Origins of Liberty: Political and Economic Liberalization in the Modern World*, P.W. Drake and M.D. McCubbins, Eds. Princeton, NJ: Princeton University Press.

Henderson, C. 1998. *Asia Falling?: Making Sense of the Asian Currency Crisis and its Aftermath*. Singapore: McGraw-Hill.

Heo, U. and S. Kim. 2000. Financial Crisis in South Korea: Failure of the Government Led Development Paradigm. *Asian Survey* 40(3):492–507.

Hicken, A. 1999. Political Parties and Linkage: Strategic Coordination in Thailand. Based on a paper prepared for delivery at the 1999 Annual Meeting of the American Political Science Association, Sept. 2–5.

———. 2001. Parties, Policy and Patronage: Governance and Growth in Thailand. In *Corruption: The Boom and Bust of East Asia*, J.E.L. Campos, Ed. Manila: Ateneo de Manila Press.

Huang, Y. 1997. The Economic and Political Integration of Hong Kong: Implications for Business Government Relations. In *Hong Kong Under Chinese Rule: The Economic and Political Implications of Reversion*, W.I. Cohen and L. Zhao. New York: Cambridge University Press.

Bibliography

Huff, W.G. 1997. *The Economic Growth of Singapore: Trade and Development in the Twentieth Century*. New York: Cambridge University Press.

Hutchcroft, P.D. 1998a. *Booty Capitalism: The Politics of Banking in the Philippines*. Ithaca, NY: Cornell University Press.

———. 1998b. Sustaining Economic and Political Reform: The Challenges Ahead. In *The Philippines: New Directions in Domestic Policy and Foreign Relations*, D. Timberman, Ed. Singapore: Asia Society.

———. 1999. Neither Dynamo nor Domino: Reforms and Crises in the Philippine Political Economy. In *The Politics of the Asian Economic Crisis*, T.J. Pempel, Ed. Ithaca, NY: Cornell University Press.

Intal, P.S. and G.M. Llanto. 1998. *Financial Reform and Development in the Philippines, 1980–1997: Imperatives, Performance and Challenges*. Manila: Philippine Institute for Development Studies.

Intal, P., M. Milo, C. Reyes and L. Basilio. 1998. The Philippines. In *East Asia in Crisis: From Being a Miracle to Needing One?* R.H. McLeod and R. Garnaut, Eds. London: Routledge.

International Monetary Fund. 1998. *World Economic Outlook* (www.imf.org).

Jaung, H. 2000. Electoral Politics and Political Parties. In *Institutional Reform and Democratic Consolidation in Korea*, L. Diamond and D.C. Shin. Stanford, CA: Hoover Institution Press.

Jayasuriya, K. 2000. Authoritarian Liberalism, Governance and the Emergence of the Regulatory State in Post-Crisis East Asia. In *Politics and Markets in the Wake of the Asian Crisis*, R. Robinson, M. Beeson, K. Jayasuriya, and H.-R. Kim, Eds. London: Routledge.

Johnston, R.B. 1991. Distressed Financial Institutions in Thailand: Structural Weaknesses, Support Operations, and Consequences. In *Banking Crises: Cases and Issues*, V. Sundararajan and T. Balino, Eds. Washington, D.C: International Monetary Fund.

Johnston, R.B., Swinburne, M., Kyei, A., Laurens, B., Mitchem, D. Otker, I., Sosa, S., and Tamarisa, N. 1999. *Exchange Rate Arrangements and Currency Convertibility: Development and Issues*. Washington, D.C.: International Monetary Fund.

Jomo, K.S. 1996. Elections' Janus Face: Limitations and Potential in Malaysia. In *The Politics of Elections in Southeast Asia*, R.H. Taylor, Ed. Cambridge: Wilson and Cambridge.

———. 1998. Malaysia: From Miracle to Debacle. In *Tigers in Trouble*, K.S. Jomo, Ed. New York: Zed Books.

Kaminsky, G.L. and C.M. Reinhart. 1998. The Twin Crises: The Causes of Banking and Balance-of-Payments Problems. Manuscript.

Kang, D. 2002. Money, Politics and the Development State in Korea. *International Organization* 56(1):177–208.

Keefer, P. 2001. Banking Crises and the Effect of Political Checks and Balances on Interest Group Influence (http://econ.worldbank.org/files/1402_wps2543.pdf).

Keefer, P. and D. Stasavage. 2003. The Limits of Delegation: Veto Players, Central Bank Independence, and the Credibility of Monetary Policy. *American Political Science Review* 47(3):389–403.

147

Kim, B.-K. 2000a. Electoral Politics and Economic Crisis, 1997–1998. In *Consolidating Democracy in South Korea*, L. Diamond and B.-K. Kim, Eds. Boulder, CO: Lynne Rienner.

————. 2000b. Party Politics in South Korea's Democracy: The Crisis of Success. In *Consolidating Democracy in South Korea*, L. Diamond and B.-K. Kim, Eds. Boulder, CO: Lynne Rienner.

Kim, E.M. 2000. Reforming the Chaebols. In *Institutional Reform and Democratic Consolidation in Korea*, L. Diamond and D.C. Shin, Eds. Stanford, CA: Hoover Institution Press.

Kim, Y.-H. 1998. Korea. In *Political Party Systems and Democratic Development in East and Southeast Asia, Vol. II*, W. Sachsenröder and U.E. Frings, Eds. Aldershot, Hampshire, UK: Ashgate.

King, D. 1999. Thailand. In *Democracy, Governance and Economic Performance: East and Southeast Asia*, I. March, J. Blondel, and T. Inoguchi, Eds. Tokyo: United Nations University Press.

Kirk, D. 1999. *Korean Crisis: Unraveling of the Miracle in the IMF Era*. New York: Palgrave.

Krugman, P. 1994. The Myth of Asia's Miracle. *Foreign Affairs* 73(6):62–78.

————. 1998a. *Currency Crises* (http://web.mit.edu/krugman/www/crises.html).

————. 1998b. The Confidence Game. *The New Republic* 219(14):23–25.

————. 1998c. *What Happened to Asia?* (http://web.mit.edu/krugman/www/DISINTER.html).

Kunio, Y. 1994. *The Nation and Economic Growth: The Philippines and Thailand*. New York: Oxford University Press.

Lamberte, M.B. 1999. *Currency Crisis: Where Do We Go from Here?* Manila: Philippine Institute for Development Studies.

Lamberte, M.B. and J.T. Tap. 1999. *Scenarios for Economic Recovery: The Philippines*. Manila: Philippine Institute for Development Studies.

Lauridsen, L.S. 1998. Thailand: Causes, Conduct, Consequences. In *Tigers in Trouble: Financial Governance, Liberalisation and Crises in East Asia*, K. S. Jomo Hong Kong: Hong Kong University Press.

Lee, Y.J. 2000. The Rise and Fall of Kim Young Sam's Embedded Reformism. In *Institutional Reform and Democratic Consolidation in Korea*, L. Diamond and D.C. Shin, Eds. Stanford, CA: Hoover Institution Press.

Leones, E. and M. Moraleda. 2000. Philippines. In *Political Party Systems and Democratic Development in East and Southeast Asia: Volume I*, W. Sachsenröder and U.E. Frings, Eds. Aldershot, Hampshire, UK: Ashgate.

Leung, E. 2000. Bank Deposit Insurance System in the Philippines (www.pdic.gov.ph).

Li, R. 2003. Banking Problems: Hong Kong's Experience in the 1980s (http://www.bis.org/publ/plcy06d.pdf).

Lim, L. 1999. Free Market Fancies: Hong Kong, Singapore, and the Asian Financial Crisis. In *The Politics of the Asian Economic Crisis*, T.J. Pempel, Ed. Ithaca, NY: Cornell University Press.

Lindblad, J.T. 1997. Survey of Recent Developments. *Bulletin of Indonesian Economic Studies* 33(3):3–34.

Bibliography

Looi, T.G. 1987. Occasional Paper No. 3: Banking Regulation and Supervision in Malaysia. Dissertation, University College of North Wales, Bangor.

MacIntyre, A. 1999a. Indonesia. In *Democracy, Governance and Economic Performance: East and Southeast Asia*, I. March, J. Blondel, and T. Inoguchi, Eds. Tokyo: United Nations University Press.

———. 1999b. Political Institutions and the Economic Crisis in Thailand and Indonesia. In *The Politics of the Asian Economic Crisis*, T.J. Pempel, Ed. Ithaca, NY: Cornell University Press.

———. 2001. The Politics of the Economic Crisis in Southeast Asia. *International Organization* 55(1):81–122.

———. 2002. *The Power of Institutions*. Ithaca, NY: Cornell Univesity Press.

Maxfield, S. 1997. *Gatekeepers of Growth: The International Political Economy of Central Banking in Developing Countries*. Princeton, NJ: Princeton University Press.

McCargo, D. 1997. Thailand's Political Parties: Real, Authentic and Actual. In *Political Change in Thailand: Democracy and Participation*, K. Hewison, Ed. London: Routledge.

McCubbins, M. 1991. Party Governance and US Budget Deficits: Divided Government and Fiscal Stalemate. In *Politics and Economics in the Eighties*, A. Alesina and G. Carliner, Eds. Chicago: University of Chicago Press.

McKinnon, R.I. and H. Pill. 1996. Credible Liberalizations and International Capital Flows: The "Overborrowing Syndrome." In *Financial Deregulation and Integration in East Asia*, T. Ito and A.O. Krueger, Eds. Chicago: University of Chicago Press.

———. 1997. Credible Economic Liberalizations and Overborrowing. *The American Economic Review* 87(2):189–93.

———. 1998. Indonesia. In *East Asia in Crisis: From Being a Miracle to Needing One?*, R.H. McLeod and R. Garnaut, Eds. London: Routledge.

Milne, R.S. and D.K. Mauzy. 1999. *Malaysian Politics under Mahathir*. London: Routledge.

Merill Lynch Co. 1998. *Banking Sector Report*. Hong Kong: Merill Lynch.

Milner, H. 1997. *Interests, Institutions, and Information*. Princeton, NJ: Princeton University Press.

Mingsarn, K.-A. 1998. Economic Development and Institutional Failures in Thailand. *TDRI Quarterly Review* (March).

Miranda, F.B. 1996a. Understanding Financial Crises: A Developing Country Perspective. In *Annual World Bank Conference on Development Economics 1996*, M. Bruno and B. Pleskovic, Eds. Washington, D.C: World Bank, pp. 29–62.

———. 1996b. Asymmetric Information and Financial Crises: A Developing Country Perspective. Paper presented at IMF Research Department Seminar, March 27.

———. 1997. Political Economy in a Democratizing Philippines: A People's Perspective. In *Democratization: Philippine Perspectives*, F. B. Miranda, Ed. Dilimoan, Quezon City: University of the Philippines Press.

———. 1999. Global Financial Instability: Framework, Events, Issues. *Journal of Economic Perspectives* 13(4):2–20.

Monetary Authority of Singapore. 1998. *Annual Report (1997/98)*. Singapore: Monetary Authority of Singapore.

Montes, M.J. 1999. The Philippines as an Unwitting Participant in the Asian Economic Crisis. In *Asian Contagion: The Causes and Consequences of a Financial Crisis*, K.D. Jackson, Ed. Boulder, CO: Westview.

Moon, C.-I. and S.-M. Kim. 2000. Democracy and Economic Performance in South Korea. In *Consolidating Democracy in South Korea*, L. Diamond and B.-K. Kim, Eds. Boulder, CO: Lynne Rienner.

———. 2001. The Politics of Economic Rise and Decline in South Korea. In *Understanding Korean Politics*, S.H. Kil and C.-I. Moon. Albany: State University of New York Press.

Mutalib, H. 1997. Singapore's First Elected Presidency: The Electoral Motivations. In *Managing Political Change in Singapore: The Elected Presidency*, K. Tan and L.P. Er, Eds. New York: Routledge.

Noble, G.W. and J. Ravenhill. 2001. Causes and Consequences of the Asian Financial Crisis. In *The Asian Financial Crisis and the Architecture of Global Finance*, G.W. Noble and J. Ravenhill, Eds. New York: Cambridge University Press, pp. 1–35.

North, D.C. and B.R. Weingast. 1991. The Evolution of Institutions Governing Public Choice in Seventeenth Century England. *Journal of Economic History* 49:803–32.

Nukul Commission Report. 1998. Bangkok: The Nation.

Obstfeld, M. 1994. The Logic of Currency Crises. *Cahier Economique et Monetaire* 43:189–213.

———. 1996. Models of Currency Crises With Self Fulfilling Features. *European Economic Review* 40:1037–47.

———. 1998. The Global Capital Market: Benefactor or Menace? *Journal of Economic Perspectives* 12(4):9–30.

Oh, J.K.C. 1999. *Korean Politics*. Ithaca, NY: Cornell University Press.

Park, C.-W. 2000. Legislative-Executive Relations and Legislative Reform. In *Institutional Reform and Democratic Consolidation in Korea*, L. Diamond and D.C. Shin, Eds. Stanford, CA: Hoover Institution Press.

Park, Y.C. 1998. *Financial Liberalization and Opening in East Asia: Issues and Policy Challenges*. Seoul: Korea Institute of Finance.

Pasuk, P. and C. Baker. 1995. *Thailand's Economy and Politics*. Bangkok: Oxford University Press.

———. 1997. Power in Transition: Thailand in the 1990s. In *Political Change in Thailand: Democracy and Participation*, K. Hewison, Ed. London: Routledge.

———. 1998. *Thailand's Boom and Bust*. Chiang Mai: Silkworm Books.

Radelet, S. and J. Sachs. 1998. *The Onset of the East Asian Financial Crisis* (http://pages.stern.nyu.edu/~nroubini/asia/).

Reisen, H. 1998. Domestic Causes of Currency Crises: Policy Lessons for Crisis Avoidance. Technical Paper No. 136. Paris: Organization for Economic Cooperation and Development.

Rodan, G. 1989. *The Political Economy of Singapore's Industrialization*. Kuala Lumpur: McMillan Press.

Bibliography

_____. 2001. Singapore: Globalization and the Politics of Economic Restructuring. In *The Political Economy of South-East Asia: Conflicts, Crises, and Change*, P.B. Kenon, Ed. New York: Oxford University Press.

Rodrik, D. 1998a. Symposium on Globalization in Perspective: An Introduction. *Journal of Economic Perspectives* 12(4):3–6.

_____. 1998b. Who Needs Capital-Account Convertibility? In *Should the IMF Pursue Capital-Account Convertibility?* Essays in International Finance No. 207, P.B. Kenon, Ed. Princeton, NJ: Princeton University Press.

Rogoff, K. 1999. International Institutions for Reducing Global Financial Instability. *Journal of Economic Perspectives* 13(4):21–42.

Rose-Ackerman, S. 1999. *Corruption and Government: Causes, Consequences, and Reform.* New York: Cambridge University Press.

Roubini, Nouriel and Jeffrey Sachs. 1989. Government Spending and Budget Deficits in the Industrial Democracies. Working Paper 2919. National Bureau of Economic Research, Cambridge, MA.

Schwarz, A. 1994. *A Nation in Waiting: Indonesia in the 1990s.* St. Leonards, NSW, Australia: Allen & Unwin.

Sheng, A. 1996. Malaysia's Bank Restructuring, 1985–1988. In *Bank Restructuring: Lessons from the 1980's*, A. Sheng, Ed. Washington, D.C.: The World Bank.

Smith, H. 1998. Korea. In *East Asia in Crisis: From Being a Miracle to Needing One?*, R.H. McLeod and R. Garnaut, Eds. London: Routledge.

So, A.Y. 1997. Contested Democracy. In *The Challenge of Hong Kong's Reintegration with China*, M.K. Chan, Ed. Hong Kong: Hong Kong University Press.

Soesastro, H. and M.C. Basri. 1998. Survey of Recent Developments. *Bulletin of Indonesian Economic Studies* 34(1):3–54.

Stiglitz, J. 1998a. Bad Private Sector Decisions. *Wall Street Journal*, Feb. 4.

_____. 1998b. Sound Finance and Sustainable Development in Asia. Keynote address to the Asia Development Forum, Manilla, Philippines, March 12, 1998.

Teik, K.B. 1995. *The Paradoxes of Mahathirism.* New York: Oxford University Press.

Tesoro, J.M. 1999. Not a Pretty Picture. *Asiaweek* 25(18): 57–60.

Thillainathan, R. 1998. The Current Malaysian Banking & Debt Crisis and the Way Forward. Expanded version of a paper delivered at ADB/World Bank Senior Policy Seminar, Manilla, Philippines, March 10.

Thompson, M.R. 1995. *The Anti-Marcos Struggle.* New Haven, CT: Yale University Press.

Tsebelis, G. 1995. Veto Players and Law Production in Parliamentary Democracies. In *Parliaments and Majority Rule in Western Europe*, H. Doring, Ed. New York: St. Martin's Press.

_____. 2002. *Veto Players: How Political Institutions Work.* Princeton, NJ: Princeton University Press.

United States Embassy in Singapore. 1998. Singapore Banking Industry Report (www.usembassysingapore.org.sg/ep/1998/bank.98.html).

Vajragupta, Y. and P. Vichayanond. 1998. *Thailand's Financial Evolution and the 1997 Crisis.* Bangkok: Thailand Development Research Institute Foundation.

Velasco, R. 1997. Does the Philippine Congress Promote Democracy? In *Democratization: Philippine Perspectives*, F.B. Miranda, Ed. Dilimoan, Quezon City: University of the Philippines Press.

———. 1999. The Philippines. In *Democracy, Governance and Economic Performance: East and Southeast Asia*, I. March, J. Blondel, and T. Inoguchi, Eds. Tokyo: United Nations University Press.

Wade, R. and F. Veneroso. 1998. The Asian Crisis: The High Debt Model Versus the Wall Street–Treasury–IMF Complex. *New Left Review* 228:3–23.

Walsh, C.E. 1998. *Monetary Theory and Policy*. Cambridge, MA: MIT Press.

Warr, P.G. 1998. Thailand. In *East Asia in Crisis: From Being a Miracle to Needing One?*, edited by R.H. McLeod and R. Garnaut. London: Routledge.

Weder, B. 1999. *Model, Myth, or Miracle?* Tokyo: United Nations University Press.

Winters, J. 1996. *Power in Motion: Capital Mobility and the Indonesian State*. Ithaca, NY: Cornell University Press.

World Bank. 1993. *The East Asian Miracle*. New York: Oxford University Press.

Young, A. 1994. Lessons from the East Asian NICs: A Contrarian View. *European Economic Review* 38(3):964–73.

Yue, C.S. 1999. The Asian Financial Crisis: Singapore's Experience and Response. In *South East Asia's Economic Crisis: Origins, Lessons, and the Way Forward*, H.W. Arndt and H. Hill, Eds. Singapore: Institute of South East Asian Studies.

Interviews by the Author

Ammar, Siamwalla. Thai Development Research Institute. Bangkok, Thailand. June 21, 1999.

Ariff, Mohamed. Executive Director, Malaysia Institute of Economic Research. Kuala Lumpur, Malaysia. June 9, 1999.

Canlas, Dante. Professor, University of the Philippines School of Economics. Manila, Philippines. May 31, 1999.

Effendi, Reno. Economist, Danareksa. Jakarta, Indonesia. June 16, 1998.

Ghosh, Ranjit. Vice President, Citibank. Bangkok, Thailand. June 30, 1999.

Gochoco-Bautista, Maria Socorro. Professor, University of the Philippines School of Economics. Manila, Philippines. May 31, 1999.

Guinigundo, Diwa. Director, Department of Economic Research, Bangko Sentral ng Pilipinas. Manila, Philippines. May 25, 1999.

Hong, Choi Siew. Chairman, Pacific Bank. Kuala Lumpur, Malaysia. June 17, 1999.

IMF Interviews. (Three officials: not for attribution.) May 13–15, 1998.

Jomo, Kwame Sundaram. Professor, University of Malaysia. Kuala Lumpur, Malaysia. June 17, 1999.

Lamberte, Mario. Officer-in-Charge, Philippine Institute for Development Studies. Manila, Philippines. May 25, 1999.

Lamberte, Mario. Officer-in-Charge, Philippine Institute for Development Studies. Manila, Philippines. E-mail communication. May 25, 2000.

Leung, Ernest. President, Philippine Deposit Insurance Corporation. Manila, Philippines. June 3, 1999.

Lin, Che Wei. Research Department (Banking). Socgen-Crosby Research Ltd. Jakarta, Indonesia. June 15, 1998.

Lirio, Riccardo. Managing Director, Bangko Sentral ng Pilipinas. Manila, Philippines. May 31, 1999.

Malhotra, Kamal. Director, Focus on the Global South. Bangkok, Thailand. July 1, 1999.

Moghadem Reza. Representative, International Monetary Fund. Bangkok, Thailand. June 10, 1998.

Paderanga, Cayetano. Member of the Monetary Board, Bangko Sentral ng Pilipinas. Manila, Philippines. E-mail communication. September 7, 1999.

153

Paderanga, Cayetano. Member of the Monetary Board, Bangko Sentral ng Pilipinas. Manila, Philippines. E-mail communication. March 21, 2000.

Paderanga, Cayetano. Member of the Monetary Board, Bangko Sentral ng Pilipinas. Manila, Philippines. E-mail communication. May 6, 2000.

Pietersz, Sriyan. Executive Director, Head of Research, Socgen-Crosby Research Ltd. Bangkok, Thailand. June 11, 1998.

Rajandram, D. Chairman, Rating Agency Malaysia. Kuala Lumpur, Malaysia. May 25, 1998.

Rajandram, D. Chairman, Rating Agency Malaysia. Kuala Lumpur, Malaysia. June 15, 1999.

Ravalo, Johnny Noe. Chief Economist. Bankers Association of the Philippines. Manila, Philippines. June 2, 1999.

Ravalo, Johnny Noe. Chief Economist. Bankers Association of the Philippines. Manila, Philippines. E-mail communication. June 15, 2000.

Ravalo, Johnny Noe. Chief Economist. Bankers Association of the Philippines. Manila, Philippines. E-mail communication. June 18, 2000.

Rustia, Andres. Managing Director, Bangko Sentral ng Pilipinas. Manila, Philippines. May 24, 1999.

Supavud, Saicheua. Executive Vice President, Merrill Lynch Phatra Securities Company Ltd. Bangkok, Thailand. June 30, 1999.

Thillainathan, R. President, Malaysian Economic Association. Kuala Lumpur, Malaysia. May 25, 1998.

Valedepenas, Dr. Vicente. Member of the Monetary Board, Bangko Sentral ng Pilipinas. Manila, Philippines. May 24, 1999.

van der Linde, Harald. Manager, Research Department, SBC Warburg Dillon Read. Jakarta, Indonesia. June 16, 1998.

Vichayanond, Dr. Pakorn. Research Director (Financial Markets), Thai Development Research Institute. Bangkok, Thailand. June 21, 1999.

Waiquamdee, Dr. Atchana. Director Economic Research Department, Bank of Thailand. Bangkok, Thailand. June 29, 1999.

Index